Makers & Monsters

Makers & Monsters

FINDING YOUR INNER ARTIST. FIGHTING YOUR INNER CRITIC.

JOSH WHITE

To those with thirsty souls and monstrous spirits.

Contents

Forward

No one taught me how to daydream.

No one taught me how to pretend that I was Batman when I wore my special Batman underwear as a child (don't judge me).

No one taught me how to draw outside the lines.

It's like I was born to do this. To dream. To imagine. Or to draw outside the lines.

What if we were born to be a maker? What if all of us were wired for wonder and created to create? What if the restlessness you feel within you is because your soul, or what I call "the real you inside of you," will always cry out for more if you live your life imitating instead of creating?

That craving of your soul and that tension you feel to be a maker is what this book, Makers & Monsters, exists to speak too. This book is not for the faint of heart, but for those willing to pioneer the right kind of anarchy. The kind that no longer accepts trading creativity for conformity and will not settle for becoming a carbon copy of someone else when they were born to be a one of a kind original.

This book is for those who would say that deep in your bones you know that your life is the greatest work of art that you will leave behind and you are determined to leave a masterpiece. This book is for the makers with the audacity, stubbornness and courage to face their monsters.

Every maker will face some for of a monster on the path to their destiny. Some of those monsters will sound like the voices of critics. Other monsters will knock on your door dressed up as depression and anxiety. Often the greatest monster, the one that can intimidate us the most, is ourselves.

The reality is that every maker will face some monsters.

The question is, do you have the audacity, stubbornness and courage to face those monsters?

The reason I am so excited about this book and can trust Josh White on the front lines of this fight for creativity is because Josh is a maker that, as you will soon read, has faced his share of monsters and has been victorious. He'll be the first to admit that he has walked away with some scars in the process, but those scars have become stories of hope that you and I need to hear as we seek to unleash the maker within us.

As Josh leads us on this journey, you will likely be comforted in the areas of challenge, but I am also sure that you will be challenged in areas you've gotten comfortable. I won't promise this adventure you're about to embark on will be easy, but I can promise it will be worth it. This will not be a book full of lame platitudes that you've read one time on an inspirational poster with a Bald Eagle on it that tells you to "dare to soar." Rather, Josh writes from a place of authenticity and vulnerability as he invites you into a life that is free from the monsters that have been lurking in the closet of your mind for far too long.

My friends, the question is not, are you a maker? You are. You were created for this.

The question is, will you decide to live in rhythm with who you were created to be? Will you decide to be a maker in a world full of people who are drawing inside the lines?

If so, then get ready.

Because the journey towards the best version of life….the truest version of life…begins on the next page. *1

- Travis Clark, Lead Pastor of Canvas SF

CHAPTER ONE:
A Call to War

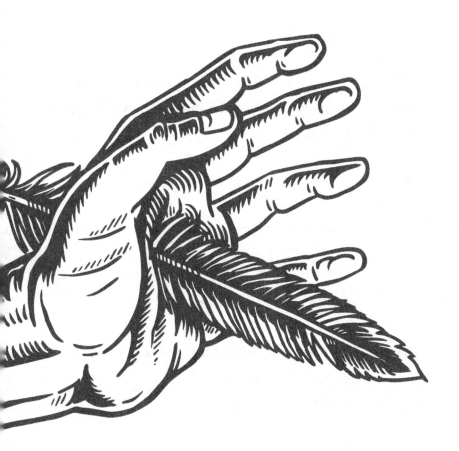

"You will never be good enough."

I can't begin to tell you how many times I've heard that.

Not from other people.

Not from outside opinions.

But from myself.

It's the one phrase that will throw my endeavors, creations, and purpose into the fiery furnace of defeat, never to see the light of day ever again.

That voice… I'm sometimes afraid of hearing that voice.

Because that voice has said some pretty damaging stuff in the past.

"They are better than you can ever be."

"That number on the scale will never go down."

"You're not as attractive as them."

"You'll never find love."

"You are broken beyond repair."

Can I ask you something?

Are you sitting there, saying to yourself, *"Yes, I've heard that voice too."*

For all of us, there has been a time when the inner critic inside of you has crept out of the dark corners of your heart to tell you something that has brought insecurity, lies, and falsehood to your calling in life.

I firmly believe that no matter what you do in this life, your biggest struggles will stem from the deepest, darkest corners of yourself.

Simply put, you are your worst enemy.

And that inner critic inside of you will always have something to say…and it's usually not a good thing.

For me, that voice went into full action on October 7th, 2015.

October 7th, 2015 was supposed to be a good day. Mainly because I had written a book that was suppose to launch on October 7th, 2015.

That book ended up in the trash. *2

You see, when it comes to writing content for others, the innate blend of an insecure perfectionist and catharsis tends to swell up so deeply inside of me that it consumes every portion of the words I put from pen to paper. And in this regard, I had to put away the perfectionist and look at the bare bones of the book I had written with a very simplistic viewpoint. That viewpoint being, "what are you even trying to say?"

There was that voice inside of me saying "this book you wrote; it's just not good enough."

And when that happened, I completely disconnected from the world. I started to re-consider what I was writing, why I was writing it, and how it would be distributed. I laid out every single sheet of the book on a table. I looked at what I was saying with honest eyes. And it was at that point that I realized I was not saying what needed to be said.

That inner voice was a monster. And it was putting this maker in check.

That Monster made me pull the plug on my book, and it looked like my insecurity and perfectionism had won the battle over the things I create.

However...that inner voice backfired on itself.

Yes, I did pull the plug on the book because I felt like it wasn't good enough. So what did I do? I wrote a new book on not being good enough.

And that's the book you are holding today.

You see, during the time that I realized that my book wasn't "good enough," I had another voice inside of me saying "it's time to put your monsters in your corner, and utilize them to create something worth creating."

The voice of the Maker started telling me to write a book explaining the inner conflicts we have as we pursue a life that's called to create.

On October 7th, 2015, I realized how to control the monster of perfectionism and become a maker of writing with complete authenticity.

Simplistically, I ended up writing an entire book that did not rally around the things in which I am called to write upon.

I stopped looking at my writing from 10-feet away, and when I did so, I realized what needed to be written. I write stories that, for me, are thoughts on my worst of days and on my best of days. I then give those stories to people to read.

The flip side of that coin is that if you're like me and you're varsity level at insecurity, then stories likes this can be extremely cathartic. My hope is that when you read the papers I pen, I want you to be able to say to yourself, "Wow. I'm not the only one."

When I realized that this is who I am as a writer, I started writing a new book on October 7th, 2015, called *Makers & Monsters*.

That was my journey of finding my inner artist and fighting my inner conflicts. However, it would be foolish of me to say that I've got it all figured out.

And I have a feeling you're right there with me.

This book contains truths and questions that you need to hear. A book that says what needs to be said. For the next handful of chapters, we're going to go on a journey together that lets you into the deepest, darkest corners of a Makers soul, and lets you into the fight that is *the artist vs. the critic*; the fight that is also known as *You Vs. Yourself.*

What you'll find in this book is stories of creation and conflict, and how those two things can turn your life into a beautiful, wonderful, artistic mess.

So whoever you are: a leader of a church, a starving artist in New York City, or a stay-at-home mom with 4 screaming children, this book is for you. You may not label yourself as "a maker," and that's totally cool…but take this journey with the rest of us. Because you just may find out that Jesus has called you to create something amazing with your life, and you most likely are already doing so without realizing it.

This is a book for leaders who want to lead well.

This is a book for those who are anxious about the next door of life.

This is a book for people who have decided to take the path less taken.

This is a book for those who want to bury the mundane of their life and dive into the deep end of their calling.

The is a book for the broken.

This is a book for the hurting.

For those who are looking for direction for their lives.

For those who want to be able to say "I will make it.

For those I want to be able to say "I made it."

For those who understand there's no such thing as "making it."

For those who have no hope.

This is a book for people who feel like they are makers.

This is a book for those who feel like they are monsters.

My hope is that this book will make you think. To create conflict. To constantly evaluate if the art you create is worth merit. This is intended for you to search deep into yourself. This book may force you to look at the parts of your life you have hidden away from yourself. And the intentionality behind this concept is not one to create more self-doubt, but rather, a beautiful moment of refinement.

Oh, and in case we've never met, I'd like to introduce myself really quick:

Hey. Name's Josh. How you doing?

Cool. Glad your day is going well. Or, sorry your day has sucked so much.

Okay, glad we got that out of the way.

You're may read things that I think many Christians are afraid of saying out loud. My spirit is to reduce the Christian elephant in the room when it comes to talking about the heart and artistry. You may disagree with what I write, or even become angry at my writings and some of the things I say and how I say them. That's fine. I hope we can still be friends.

I also consider myself an artist. I'm someone who looks for the beauty and creativity in all aspects of their life. I live to make art, whether that be by music, writings, relationships, experiences, and empowering new leaders.

You might not be a follower of Jesus. You might not label yourself as a creative. You may have gotten his book from a friend and you're only reading this because they asked you to. There are no qualifications to reading or understanding the words in this book. But trust me, if you dive into this book with everything you've got, I promise that you will be able to see your life in a more authentic way.

My hope is that this book will show you what love is. What type of beauty pain can bring. What joy creativity can hold for your life. What it means to completely push yourself into the path you thought you were supposed to follow.

What it means to be a maker.

What it means to embrace your monsters.

Remember October 7th, 2015? That was the day the book before this one was supposed to be published. I distinctly remember what that night was like. That night was suppose to be a party night. A feeling of tumultuous joy celebrating a finished work. However, that night turned into one of the deepest, darkest discussions I have ever had with my soul.

I spent that night, along with the days following contemplating whether or not I should publish the words from my journal. I mean, we're talking about some pretty heavy things here, even to the point that some people may not understand or just end up thinking I was crazy. I knew one thing was certain: I knew the season of being a writer was not suppose to be over, but the inner struggle I continued to have with myself was how to produce words that Josh felt was worth something.

That Josh felt was worth something.
That JOSH felt was worth something.

That right there is the inner battle I have with myself each and every day. The battle that what I create is never good enough.

What about you? Have you ever felt this way? No matter what you touch, what you do, what you create, who you influence, is that still small voice inside of you still saying, *"that was not good enough."*

You may lie to yourself and say you've conquered that voice.

But let me tell you right now, that voice is a monster.

Finding who you are as a maker is exciting. Battling your monsters can hurt. This book is a journey of words and emotions, and I hope that as we walk through this together you will be challenged to become the maker that The Maker intended you to be.

To start our crazy journey of finding your inner artist and fighting your inner critics, I want to take you back to my childhood for a couple minutes. Specifically, the first time I ever told myself "you will never be good enough."

I was 8 years old, and I stood in the locker room staring at my reflection in the mirror. I quickly wiped the tears from my eyes as a group of boys walked in. I left quietly and headed to my classroom. I had just left P.E. class, where I came in last during a one-mile run. I remember passing the finish line with sweat stinging my eyes as it poured down from my forehead.

The rest of the class was already gone by the time I arrived at the locker room. I sat on a cold bench, thinking to myself, "why can't you just be faster?"

Once I left the locker room, I slowly composed myself for next period: lunch.

Something was different about this day. I remember sitting at the end of an empty table. I unzipped my lunchbox, sat there quietly, and ate a peanut butter and jelly sandwich with the company of myself.

These moments were part of an ongoing battle in my head and heart. As you read that story, did you say to yourself, *"Man...this sounds familiar."* I have a feeling you have had these thoughts, just like me.

I tell you this story to remind you that you are not alone.

Listen to me.

You are not alone.

The reason why you have these thoughts is because of one simple fact. You're human.

And humans aren't perfect.

For years, I felt the need to hide my inner struggles from people, because they were ugly and embarrassing. They didn't contribute anything to the world or those in it. And for quite some time, I would showcase one life for the public, and then privately create one for my authentic self, because I was under the assumption that who I really was wasn't good enough for people to see. I would put a smile on my face while there was fear in my heart.

I would say one thing because that's what I felt like they wanted to hear. As an artist, I felt that my fake personality was starting to creep into my artistry. I would sing one way and listen to a certain genre of music when I knew I didn't care for it. I would create things because they were popular, not because that's the type of artist I am.

And to this day, I fight this battle with myself: the battle to make everything I say, create, lead, and pray truly authentic to who I am.

Ask yourself, "Do I fight this battle too?"

If you do…then welcome to the civil war of fighting your monsters.

Every artist to some degree is a perfectionist - and by a perfectionist, I mean a very specific type of perfection. It doesn't mean they always want the right words, the straightest lines, or the perfect color - they want their message to have validity. If we were honest, that is truly the artists greatest fear - the fear that what they create won't hold any value to anyone, including themselves.

But what I have realized is that the darker parts of my life are the ones that are most applicable to those around me. They don't want what I think they want. They want to hear the message inside of me, because more than likely, they are hiding the same message inside of them. Because of this, I started letting people into the deepest, darkest corners of my life. I would let them experience just how "awful" Josh really was. And people started listening. They would read what I would write. They would listen to words I would type. And I believe they would listen because the words I was saying were truly authentic.

Because of my monsters, I found my inner artist.

Friend: you have a story worth telling. You have life paths that have given you emotional scars, but those scars framed who you are today. And while you may have some scars from the past, you may also be currently fighting those battles.

For some of us, we're fighting battles with depression.

With divorce.

With Obesity. Inadequacy. Motherhood. Cancer. Loneliness.

Here's the awesome thing: these are all monsters than we can *create* from.

Today, I'm asking you to pull the mask off and reveal who you really are. If we are to create the masterpiece that God has placed in our lives to create, we must be Makers full of transparent authenticity. Time will show us that these monsters of our past, present, and future are some of the most valuable resources in our tool belt as a Maker.

However, I also believe monsters are one of the biggest ingredients we need to become the best makers on earth.

Here's the thing about monsters: monsters like to creep up and scare us from behind. They hide in the deepest and darkest corners of your life and strike us at the most inconvenient time. Monsters keep us on our toes. Monsters can come out of nowhere. They're there for a reason. As someone who strives to live their life as creatively as possible, being aware of your monsters is one of the greatest ways you can defeat them.

The only problem is that "problems" are a monster themselves. And we fight this monster each day. Our society views problems with a dark underline, only focusing on the turmoil and chaos that problems create. Yes, life can easily scream at us sometimes; but trust me when I say, the moments that you decide to scream back are the moments when your inner critic dies, and your inner artist comes alive.

Being a maker is understanding that creating is a process that has both good and bad. Life is a series of battles of an inner war that you constantly fight with yourself. So much so, that life will bend and break you in the moments when you least expect it.

You will wake up one day, and tell yourself "this is the best I have been" and two days later, all four corners of your heart can come crashing in. Any coward can seem courageous when he's surrounded by a life that fills him up. But when you are alone and your blood runs thin, that's when you decide if you're going to let your own doubt, fear, and hurt control the foundation of who you are.

Trust me when I say, the monster of hurt can come when you least expect it, from nowhere with absolutely no reasoning.

But that hurt you feel has a deep truth attached to it.

It has refinement. And as a maker, refinement is a very valuable tool in creating.

When hurt comes into your life, you have one of two choices. The first, being that you can sit in that hurt, and let the anger and confusion of your hurt slowly erase away who you are as a person. The second being, when hurt is created into the deepest parts of who you are, you can take that hurt, and craft it into something beautiful.

Maker: choose the latter. Take your hurt, and craft it into progress.

Always remember, you were made to kill your monsters. Study your monsters. Figure out what scares them, and then crush them. The monsters in your life give you a lack of complacency. And that's exactly what they're there to do. Don't let yourself become comfortable. Comfortability equals complacency. Complacency equals status quo. Status quo equals failure. If you let risk become fear, then that means your monsters have defeated you.

At the end of the day, when all your monsters have been slain, it's important that you don't become a monster yourself. Keep yourself and your art humble. Just because you conquered today's monsters does not mean a bigger monster isn't going to come right at you tomorrow morning. Keep your work, your art, and your profession a place of humility.

I'll say it again. Monsters are there for a reason.

Do not let the monsters of your life dictate what your masterpiece will look like. Let life breathe into you a sentence, and write back a novel. Put on a sweater with a loose thread that your hope and dreams cannot resist pulling, and then pull with the fear that all may unravel around you. Give yourself a boat, mount it with the fastest sail, and take on the darkest of storms.

The nightmare that is your monsters can be your crafting tool. Where many would be scared, you can find yourself fascinated. Don't allow the shadows that surround your life engage you in frightfulness. Embrace your night, and battle your monsters.

Sure, this doesn't sound normal. The world inside of your imagination can be a twisted a dream. But that imaginative journey is what makes a Maker smile.

Monsters can make us do crazy things. But always remember, you decided to be a maker and to choose that life, you've got to be a little crazy already.

Embrace the darkness of your life.

Craft that darkness into beauty.

Whew. Okay. Glad I got that off my chest.

Are you ready for this journey? It's not going to be easy.

I'm ready to go on it with you. And during this journey, let's see if we can figure out how we can take what you think are the worst parts about you, and create something absolutely astonishing with it.

Yup, it's as crazy as it sounds.

But it's going to take a lot of work.

And a lot of fighting.

Brace yourselves, because we're about to go into war.

CHAPTER TWO:
Axes and Anchors

I hated art class.

My elementary art teacher and I didn't enjoy each other's company. I always felt like she was mad at me, and to be honest, I can't really remember what I did to make her hate me. I distinctly remember one time when I accidentally dropped my eraser on the floor and she stopped showing us how to make snowmen out of cotton balls to yell at me for playing around in class.

In my defense, the snowman project was incredibly boring. [3]

On one particular project, we were told to create a paper mâché wind chime. The instructions were simple: we were told to create a ball of paper mâché that would hang from a string which would in return knock into each other to make a sound...therefore, the wind chime. It was also early spring, so we were told to use vibrant Easter colors.

This project was just fine, outside of one overlooked issue: when banged together, paper balls do not make the sound of a wind chime. Also, I wasn't a big fan of bright colors. I wanted to paint mine dark.

Now…before we go anymore forward, you have to understand that I wasn't the greatest second grader of all time. It wasn't just my art teacher, but my other teachers would easily get frustrated at me.

It could be that I asked a lot of questions. Or maybe art just wasn't her thing. Maybe she hated children (I would too if I had to put up with me in second grade). I'm just going to say we both had a different viewpoint on artistry. The way she had us make things was always by the book. You have the instructions, the guidelines, and you do EXACTLY what the rules tell you to do. For myself, I personally enjoyed branching out a little bit more to make whatever project we were doing a little more personalized.

"Excuse me teacher, but I don't get this."

"What don't you get?"

"When you hit these paper balls together, they don't make any sound. We're making wind chimes here. They're supposed to make a sound. Oh, also, all these colors are super bright and I'd like to paint mine black."

"Just make the paper balls and paint them pink or yellow."

"But…they don't make any…"

"JUST PAINT THE BALLS YELLOW."

At this point, I was a little irritated. "Why are we even doing this project? They don't even do what a wind chime is supposed to do. They're just for decoration. They don't serve any purpose."

So, just like any strong-willed second grader would do, I took the situation into my own hands.

After making the paper mâché balls, I glued little pieces of metal that were left from a previous project all over the balls so when they hit each other they would make a sound.

I painted the balls black because I was a little stubborn child who didn't want yellow paper mâché balls. I had essentially made three giant terrifying balls that looked like they were a medieval battle weapon.

I couldn't have been happier with my creation.

I waited in anticipation as my art teacher went around to each desk, giving praises to everyone's brightly colored, dull sounding wind chimes. She then proceeded to my desk.

"…what is this."

"It's my wind chime. I decided to make a few adjustments to the…"

"Give it to me. You didn't follow instructions. You get an F and this is going in the trash."

I was completely devastated. I understood that I didn't follow the instructions the way I should have, but I firmly believed this was better than what she said to do.

"...you're going to fail me AND throw away my creation?

I spent the next 30 minutes in tears and in anger as I watched the rest of the class hit their non-chimey wind chimes together outside on the playground.

What I didn't realize at the time is that even as an 8-year-old, I was caught in the paradox of the any maker.

For anyone, whether you consider yourself an artist or not, this one thing is true about our humanity: we boldly want to pursue the fulfilled life, but too many times, we we have one too many stumbling blocks in front of us. And those stumbling makes us choose an easier, more "status-quo" life.

I didn't follow the instructions or the rules, which is why she failed me. I later apologized for my actions and regretted the fact that I didn't do what was asked. I still don't understand why she had to throw away my amazing invention in the trash can, but that's something she'll have to deal with once Jesus confronts her about it in The Kingdom (I've been thinking about that day for 20 years). The point is, I didn't follow the rules, and rules are there for a reason.

....rules are there for a reason.

For a reason.

Reason: *"a justification for an action or event processed by logic."*

One thing I have recently learned while finding my inner maker: **logic doesn't play well with creativity.**

As a maker, there are two things you must always consider while creating your masterpiece: what are the things that keep me grounded, and what are the things that hold me back?

You see, I view moments in my life as masterpieces. When an artist transfers his emotions onto a canvas, he sits back and calls it a masterpiece. The same can be true when we walk away from a project where we completed a goal, a refining moment in a relationship with someone, or simply by having a perfect day. In all walks of our life, there are things that are the foundation of our masterpieces, and there are things that we do that keep us from making masterpieces.

One of the things that keeps us from making masterpieces is having one too many tools in our tool belt. And sometimes, one of those tools is something you would think we would all want, but rather it hinders our productivity.

It's called "creative freedom."

Creativity is full of paradoxes; not the least of which is the fact that having absolute creative freedom is often highly uncreative. It's a phenomenon we call "paralysis of choice." The more options we have, the harder it is to choose anything. In return, we end up creating nothing. When everything is an option, somehow we find ourselves option-less. Which is why almost every artistic medium develops its own limitations over time.

One of my favorite authors, G. K. Chesterton once said, "The most beautiful part of every picture is the frame." What Chesterton was saying here was, in short, "art wants limits."

Sometimes, having ultimate creative freedom can actually damage our ending masterpiece. While most artist feel like rules and discipline are something that they need to cut off from their life, I would debate that rules and discipline actually are qualities that keep us grounded in our artistry.

For the next few paragraphs, I want to show you 4 creative restraints that we all can learn from.

The Exterminating Angel

I watched this really weird movie once that was filmed in 1962. It's completely in Spanish. It's a Mexican film called *The Exterminating Angel.* It's about this dinner party where the guests find themselves unable to leave the dining room in which they are eating dinner.

There's no reason they can't leave. They just can't. And while this sounds really, really weird (don't get me wrong, it really, really was), it actually held this pretty crazy storyline that didn't make sense until the very end. You see, the limitations of the story become the story. The guests are unable to leave, and because of that, I wasn't able to stop watching the movie. I had to finish it. It was almost as if I couldn't go on with life until one of them left that room.

Creative constraint 101 right here. The storyline was so, so simple, yet this movie went on to be named as The New York Times one of the 1,000 best films of all time.

The lesson here is not just about the power of constraints, but the power of arbitrary constraints. There doesn't need to be a grand design or reasoning behind the limitations you set for yourself. Sometimes you only understand their meaning once you start working inside of them.

Dr. Seuss, Minimalist

Theodor Geisel, who we know as "Dr. Seus" lost a bet with his publisher after his finished his work, *Cat in the Hat.*

As a bet with the founder of Random House, he wrote Green Eggs and Ham using just 50 different words. Fifty. Five-oh. That's it. But here's the crazy part: beyond just winning the bet, Green Eggs and Ham went on to be not only be Geisel's most popular book, but also one of the best-selling children's books ever written. If you want to inspire your wildest rule-breaking creativity, the secret (like it or not) might be setting some wildly restricting rules.

Henri Matisse, Scissor Artist

Toward the end of his life, Henri Matisse was too sick to work. Multiple surgeries and diseases had left him mostly bedridden. The great painter could no longer paint. But rather than let his limitation be the disappointing period at the end of an otherwise incandescent career, Matisse dedicated himself to a new art form: paper cutouts. During his last decade, using primarily scissors and paper, Matisse produced some of his best-known art — work he called "drawing with scissors."

His unwanted but quickly welcomed limitation was the key to an entirely new and innovative era of his art. We can't always choose our constraints, but we can always choose how we respond to them. Our response to limitations often defines us as artists.

Gadsby, the Novel with No E

Here's a case of taking limitations too far. In 1939, Earnest Vincent Wright wrote Gadsby, a novel that doesn't contain the letter E. This limitation was not only used to sell the book (a note about the limitation takes up most of the cover), but it's the only thing anybody remembers about the book.

The characters, the plot, the ideas all became secondary to a limitation that, in the end, was more schtick than anything else. The point being, while limitations can be inspiring (maybe even essential), they should never overshadow the work.

Composer Igor Stravinsky said: *"The more constraints one imposes, the more one frees one's self. And the arbitrariness of the constraint serves only to obtain precision of execution."*

Throughout history, limitations have resulted in some of the most compelling pieces of art ever produced. Limitations give our work energy. They give us boundaries to press against. And more than just a trick for overcoming writer's block, they can act as a catalyst for an entire piece of work.

In the end, the rules that constrict us set us free.

So, songwriters: stop adding measures and hooks. Keep it simple.

Writers: maybe you don't need 200 pages for the concept of your writing. Say what you need to say in 50 pages or less.

Pastors: maybe they don't need to hear every story from your past. Or maybe not every verse that pertains to your topic. Can you say what Jesus wants you to say with just one verse and one story?

Here's the flip side of the coin: when we apply this constriction to our creativity, we can easily takes rules and actually find fulfillment by checking off our creative to-do list.

And when we do that, we lose what I call our "wild."

Wild Makers and Tame Makers

We all know people that I like to call Wild Makers. It's the guy that can play any instrument with ease. The person who can pick up a pencil and draw something incredible with no training.

These creatives are born with extreme, untapped potential. They create when they don't even mean to. They produce excellence in their sleep. And the rest the creative world is sometimes frustrated with these type of people because they can accomplish in one day what would take us a year.

I know. I hate them too.

While finding and tapping into raw potential is an X-factor in any form of artistry, there's still one major aspect that many wild makers tend to forget about themselves: wild artistry is still immature and must be nurtured.

Some of the greatest artists in the world are those who have the most scars. The ones who produce, get shot down, and produce more will be the ones that will produce artistic maturity. The maker who simply produces without nurturing his or her artistry is doomed for failure.

However, this is only one side of the coin.

Then, we come across those that I call Tame Makers. Too many times, I've found Wild Makers who dictate what their artistry looks like so much that they lose the daydreamer inside of them.

They put their masterpieces on schedules. They tell their minds when to produce, when to shut off, and when it's appropriate to create. And sometimes, I've seen Tame Makers manipulate their personalities to a point where they become so complacent that they only produce content because they feel like they have to.

There's a balance between both of these personalities, and that's where you can find the Maker who is going to create masterpiece after masterpiece.

Wild Makers: don't ever lose your daydreams. However, make sure you are listening to your mentors and those around you who are helping you mature your creative art. Yes, you are a natural born artist, but those who are leading you are refining what you produce. They're not just there to make you feel bad. Listen to them. Cut out your ego. Anchor yourself in their leadership. You're not as good as you think you are, and you can create much better quality artistry if you humble yourself enough to take criticism from your leaders.

Tame Makers: you will only produce mediocre pieces of art if you tell your soul when it's time to create. The reason why you cannot create something with extraordinary value is because you are telling yourself when it's allowed to. Learn from the Wild Makers. You'll know when it's time to create. And when it's time to create, create with the matured value that you already have within yourself.

Keeping our artistry in restraint while keeping our wild inside of us is what can anchor us in creating our masterpieces. But sometimes, there are certain things we need to cut off in our lives as well, and some things we must always hold on to.

When we talk about Wild and Tame Makers, we are primarily talking about what the bi- product of our lives, which are the things we create. However, before we can even start talking about the bi-product, we have to talk about the catalyst of lives. And when a creative creates, he may have logic and intelligence behind his creations…but they always fall short unless his add emotion to the product.

And we all know our emotions are a monster in themselves.

Friends: I'll be the first to admit that life can really scream at you sometimes.

It doesn't always scream at you in the worst of ways; but sometimes, it's just enough to make your life seem a little more than what you tend to typically bare.

Life can easily decide to cut your teeth on thin ice; and no matter how strong your emotional frame may be, it can stagger above you ten feet tall, and give you no reassurance that a better life is right around the corner.

However, I also believe life screams at us at times when we need it.

I believe life is a process, and it's a process that has both good and bad.

I believe life is a series of battles of an inner war that you constantly fight with your earthly flesh.

And that's perfectly okay.

In this chapter, we've been learning about the things that we need to cut off from our lives, and the things that keep us grounded. Along with these two, I believe in two things when facing life battles: you flee, and you flock. You flee things that destroy you, and you flock to those things that grow you.

Today, I want to express to you my belief in fleeing and flocking.

First, we flee those things that need to be left behind. And sometimes, it's careers. Projects. Agendas. Things that give you false comfort. Negative thoughts that drive you down a path of false hope.

Sometimes, it's memories.

Other times, it's relationships.

We all have something that we need to flee from.

Let's stop right there for a second…

You've already got something in your head that you're saying, "yeah…for me, it's definitely this."

For all of us, there is at least one thing in our lives that you know you would be better off without…but for some reason, you hold onto it with a firm grip, as if you can never let it go. There are times when you have to let things go, even when you don't want to. Such is life. Don't try to make up a false sense of hope in keeping things that give you momentary value and satisfaction. Instead, leave the things you know you need to reject behind you. And don't ever look back.

Sometimes, It's memories that bring out the worst in you.

It's a relationship that destroys every fabric of who you are.

It's your innate dark thoughts that tell you "you will never be good enough."

My friends; flee these things. Run away from them with reckless abandon.

And don't ever look back.

And secondly, flock to those things that you need the most.

Leaving things behind is only half of the battle. And to be quite honest, sometimes leaving things behind is easier than picking up those things we need to flock towards.

Sometimes, it's a life path we're afraid of following.

A passionate goal that seems unreachable.

What your life looks like without certain people.

What it means to be a vessel of Christ instead of a vessel of You.

Flocking towards things we are pursuing can be harder than leaving things behind; but trust me when I say, the doubter inside of you will quickly dissolve once you see purpose in the things you are flocking towards. I don't believe in the status-quo life; I believe in a life that is filled with passion, purpose, order, discipline, and creativity.

And to make your life revolve around those 5 things, you have to pursue your passions, no matter what they are. Pursuit can be a scary thing; and if we were honest, the reason why we don't flock towards what we believe in is because of insecurity and discipline. Those two things will quickly kill anyone's dream. However, if you constantly flock towards your passion, those two elements of who you are will die along with the things you left behind.

Flee the fact you can't override reality. Flock towards proving the nay-sayers wrong.

Flee false hope. Flock towards grace and love.

Flee status-quo. Flock towards passionate ambition.

Flee who you are. Flock towards who you were meant to be.

Flee yourself. Flock towards grace.

As a maker, pick up your axe and cut the monsters that are holding you back from creating your masterpieces. Anchor yourself in who you are as an artist, and produce the quality work that you know you are capable of. This process takes time, but trust me, this is the best way for you to become the maker you were created to be.

"There are no rules for architecture in the clouds." -G.K. Chesterton

CHAPTER THREE:
Water and Brimstone

"Gays are nothing but fags and queers."

I will never forget the day I heard this from a pulpit, from a pastor, in a church.

Let's throw some backstory to what happened.

I grew up in the rural midwest. For years, I called Indiana home. I did what most midwest kids do; I got lost in cornfields, made tree houses in the middle of the woods, and caught lightning bugs in mason jars. I grew up with Johnny Cash and learned life values from John Wayne. There was even this one time where I got a slingshot for Christmas and got it taken away the same day because I kept breaking windows and killing pigeons.

But there was another part of my upbringing that shaped my early years of faith. I grew up in what in a denomination that calls themselves Independent Fundamental Baptists. If you're not familiar with what they are known for, here's an overview:

People inside of the IFB hold to pretty conservative beliefs. The term "independent" refers to the doctrinal position of the church. They refuse to join any affiliated convention or hierarchical structure of ministry. They twist personal convictions into theological stances. The leadership is viewed just like Jesus; God and the pastor are almost one and the same. [5]

Here's what I saw as a 7-year-old boy:

When you go to church, you wear a suit and tie, and women wear dresses. Anyone who is wearing something less is viewed as a lesser person.

No music other than hymns. If there's a song that doesn't talk about Jesus, you don't listen to it. If there's a song that uses more than just a piano, it's wrong.

America is just as holy as Jesus.

Drinking and tattoos are an abomination, and you're probably going to hell if you drink or have tattoos.

As long as I look perfect on Sunday, say the right things, and play the part, it doesn't matter what I do Monday thru Friday.

And unfortunately, these examples are only the surface level to this denomination. There was a much deeper, darker view behind the scenes of the IFB church.

I was taught that there was only a particular group of people Jesus loved. So much so, that I heard a college professor once say "I would never hire a mixed couple. I will only hire white people on my staff." During an internship at an IFB Church, I remember being told to tell someone who had a pretty dark past that they weren't allowed to sing in our choir. I remember being told to only witness to people in affluent neighborhoods, because "God loves a cheerful giver, and those under a certain annual salary can't give the way we want them to."

If I had to put into one sentence what the IFB taught me, it would be this: God only loves people who look, act and give a certain way.

I was taught to only love a certain type of person. And this never sat well with me.

This all came crashing down in my faith when I heard those words from the pulpit:

"Gays are nothing but fags and queers."

I sat there in complete disbelief. And it wasn't so much the fact that those words just came from a pastor from the pulpit.

The thing that shocked me the most was the sound of overwhelming "amens" for church-goers in the pews behind me.. It was literally one of the loudest responses to a sermon point (if you even want to call it that) I had heard in my church.

That was the first day I remember feeling indifferent about Christianity. I spent a good amount of time navigating my emotions about it. Because I had heard it from a pulpit, I was under the assumption that it was truth. I was 12 years old, and at this point in life, I had no reason to not believe a pastor or what he was saying. But because of the way it that it was delivered, it challenged my heart.

It wasn't that a man of God was labeling the homosexual community through a derogatory verbiage, even though that alone was enough for Jesus to tell me something about this wasn't right. What was challenging to me is when he said that they were nothing but a fag or a queer.

"Nothing but a fag or a queer."

As soon as I heard that, I knew something about that was not right. And as a seven-year-old, I sat there soaking in this moment knowing that this was the first time I had ever disagreed with a mentor. However... at that point in life, I couldn't tell you why I didn't agree with him. I just knew I didn't.

It took me years to figure out why I didn't agree with the hostility that was presented towards a group of people. But what I had read about God didn't line up with what he said from the pulpit. From that point on, I started questioning many things about the Independent Fundamental Baptist Church.

Fast forward 14 years.

At 21, my life came crashing down. I fell, hard. Real hard. And when I needed people around me the most, they abandoned me, because I no longer showcased what the IFB church looked like.

This event in my life catapulted me into realizing that every emotion I had towards the IFB church was true. They did not love me. They loved what I was able to do for them. They loved a fake version of me that I would show from a pulpit on a Sunday.

And during this time in my life, I remembered the day I sat in that church serve hearing those words labeling the homosexual community.

Finally, I was able to put words to why I didn't agree with that statement, or the entire IFB movement:
I was being told that love is not unconditional.

So, I ran.

I ran from everything I had learned. I ran from mentors that I trusted. I ran from this fake version of Jesus.

And when I ran, I was scolded, betrayed, and left alone. But I kept running from it. If I stayed where I was, I knew the Maker who God intended me to be would be diminished to nothing more than a cog in the machine.

People will ask me to this day why I ran, and my answer is still the same: I was being told that there was a group of people I shouldn't love. And this made more sense to me when I realized I wasn't loved by the IFB church.

And ever since I decided to leave this house of religion, the things God created me to create have been not only accepted, but authentic. Here is the glorious outcome of this 21 year battle with my beliefs: **God showed me that makers are sometimes put into houses where they cannot create what their heart is intended to make.**

I left a place that would hinder my artistry because I cannot create for only a select few people. Inside of the IFB church, I was told to only be a maker who loves and creates for affluent whites. My artistry of life had to look a specific way, even when I knew that the person I was and the things I was creating were fake.

I refused to have fake artistry.

As an artist, you will eventually come across the path where platform and authenticity collide with one another.

An artist can have success manufacturing art to attract the masses. There's one major problem with this: fake artistry can only last until the fad is over.

I've seen Tame Makers follow this path, and give up themselves for the sake of trying to attract others to their work. The artwork that comes from the soul ebbs and flows as you naturally evolve as a person. And because of this, it connects to more people – because people connect to authenticity.

You can live your life with a deep confidence because your artwork full of transparency and honesty. If you create this type of artwork, you will have nothing to ever apologize for, and you will have nothing to be self-conscious of. You are simply being the maker you were created to be. Evolving as a person spiritually, emotionally and mentally takes you deeper into the truth of who you truly are, and from that place of integrity, your truest masterpiece can be created.

However, this doesn't mean your artwork never changes. When you create from the foundation of integrity, your art will always have something special for someone. It's when we compromise integrity and artwork is when our masterpieces become diluted into a lie.

But, artists still create artwork that isn't at the foundation of their personality. Why is this? Why would we create something that doesn't hold any value to ourselves? The answers can easily vary: for money, success, fear of failure, the want to fit in, and the list goes on. What we must always remember is that creating from this will never work. We often, if not always lose in the long term by going against the very fiber of who we are as a maker.

The flip side of this situation is those who are still trying to figure out who they are. They are the Wild Makers who are still so young into their artistry that they don't even know who they are as a maker. For those Wild Makers, my response is simple: try everything. All of it. And if it connects with your soul, there is a chance you just may have found who are as an artist.

One way to begin this process of knowing who you are as a maker and aligning it with your integrity is to practice listening to your intuition as an artist. This tangible action is simple: just listening for the first gut response you have. Don't second guess it. Just create. Remove all the thoughts attached to fear. Practice following your impulses. Spearhead your first idea, and follow the artwork that lights your soul on fire.

We are all influenced by our early experiences, living, reacting and making choices based on early wounds, beliefs and learned ideas. Everyone has an idea of who they are based on a million things we've been told by our parents, teachers, siblings, friends, and even strangers. As we learn who we are as an artist, our responsibility is to either evolve or unsubscribe to ideas that come and go.

Practice knowing yourself, and aligning your actions with your integrity, passion, and purpose. Take action on your dreams and watch your life and creativity flow. But always remind yourself that the line between authenticity and being true to yourself can be forced into a false definition by the culture you surround yourself with.

This whole line between authenticity and being true to yourself reminds me of one of my friends who's a creative director at a marketing group in NYC. We're going to call him "John."

John's biggest hang-up was working on products he didn't believe in. The last thing he wanted to do was to be a sell out that sold an energy drink or a children's toy to a market that was probably already going to purchase it.

I remember John telling me this story about him being in college and absolutely hating marketing. It was never something John thought he would ever decide to go near. The main reason being, John felt like every venue of advertising was him being a sell out.

Oh. John's kinda a hippie. I forgot to tell you that.

Anyways… one day, John decided to mouth off to one of his college professors who used to be a major marketing executive before retiring and teaching at John's university.

John decided to "challenge the system" and tell his college professor that "any form of marketing is made to make someone purchase something: and it's totally one sided. You're just doing this to make me buy something that won't do anything for me, but will just make you more money."

That same college professor looked at John and said, "When you get out of here, what do you want to do with your life?

John's answer was simple: he wanted to pursue a self-employment position where he lead a team of creatives to raise funds for starving artists in Chicago, which was his home town.

John's professor said, "All those things you're talking about are technically forms of advertising. As a matter of fact, any job with a leadership position is marketing…because you have to sell your vision. Otherwise, no one is going to follow you. You have to *make* them believe you."

You see, John didn't have a realistic view of marketing before then. He didn't understand what was possible.

John didn't understand the full range of what advertising could mean. He was coming at everything from *only* a design perspective.

John finally realized that promotion was not sell-out. He explained how you can pretty much turn anything you're interested in into an advertising gig. He finally realized he had the power to make sure the correct venue was taken with his marketing.

In short, John learned that "sell-out" is what "selling-out" means to you and your integrity.

Friends: while not all of us are not design majors, but we are all marketers in some capacity. If you believe in something, you'll want to share it. And to do so, you have to explain your vision and cast that to those around you.

At the end of the day, it's finding ways to relate to people. When you watch a commercial that feels earnest or honest, it resonates. You can have these awesome moments with a brand. When you advertise, you can contribute to something valuable, not just create a bunch of nonsense that people will ignore.

John eventually graduated college and landed a job that helped cable companies take on PR issues. His first job was in Seattle to help a local coffee shop. This coffee shop had a unexpected visit from a health inspector and severely failed. When local TV stations heard about this, they jumped on the idea to capitalize on the situation for a late night story.

What the media didn't explain is that the health issues were issues that most, if not all restaurants would deal with, and they were met with a health inspector that was having a really, REALLY bad day.

So, John was hired to help the coffee shop reclaim their reputation in Seattle. John knew he had a pretty major situation in front of him, and he knew he needed to do some serious researching before even contacting the coffee shop.

But John didn't research the health situation. Instead, John started researching the culture of Seattle Washington.

"When you start researching, you realize just how different the cultures in other cities can be. How different the interests are. They might not even care about the thing you think is big in their town. You can't talk to everybody the same way. Even if the scripts are very similar, they have to be customized for the audience. You need that regional dialect. Those subtle accents. I wanted to feel like I had been born and raised in Seattle," John said.

And to figure that out about a culture…that takes work. A lot of work. You have to throw yourself into their community, be completely transparent with them, and let them express who they are to you. It's not a turn of the key by any stretch of the imagination. For these ads, John needed to do his research. He needed to scout. He had to make sure he was talking to people in an appropriate way and highlighting things about their city that would surprise them. That's what made the ads authentic.

That takes work.

That takes authentic, transparent work.

And with that work, John took something he felt was non-authentic, and made it true to himself.

If you were to ask John what the thinks of when he thinks of authenticity, he would tell you, "I think of some coffee shop barista wearing a homemade denim apron and just, like, being himself, man."

It's easy to think of authenticity as being true to yourself, but it's more about being true to your subject. If you aren't resonating with the people who are watching, then what are you doing? Just like John did with the culture to Seattle, we need to make our artistry as authentic to the people we were designed to speak to. It's been a labor of love.

And trust me, it's really rewarding.

A lot of Tame Makers end up in the wrong creative field just to make a living, but that doesn't mean we can't bring back our wild and create something worthwhile.

I didn't tell you that story about John just because he's the coolest self-labeled hippie I know. I told you that story because John went from thinking he was living a lie by marketing, and soon realized, as long as he was being true to himself, he *wanted* to tell people about the story he was promoting.

Friends: creating authentic artwork isn't easy. It takes real work. It takes researching, scouting, and listening. But in the end, it's possible to make something that not only delivers a message but also resonates with an audience.

I mean, isn't that what we're all after anyway?

At the core of an artist, we create to express a message; and any good artist doesn't want to be selfish with that message because he understands that message has tremendous value to someone outside of himself. But that takes work. That takes finding who you are as a maker. I found who I am as a maker by fleeing those that would hold back my artistry. John found his by immersing himself in promoting truth to a specific community. And John did just that for his now-favorite coffee shop in Seattle.

Now, that Seattle coffee shop is loved by more than most in its neighborhood.

How will you find who you are as a maker? Whatever experience may come your way, always keep your integrity at the forefront of your artistry. When that happens, you'll be creating masterpieces that will mirror the true Maker inside of yourself.

CHAPTER FOUR:
Kings and Humans

A conversation with a friend went like this:

"Josh, I just wish my team would produce better. Work better together."

I replied, "Are you finding areas where they shine? Are you refining the raw talent you see in them?"

He then said, "Not really...because then they'd be better than me" and then proceeded to chuckle.

When I asked him if he was serious, he went a little white in the face.

I see it far too often; the leaders who are afraid of completing the transformation in others from follower to leader because of their own ego. They fear that what they are and who they leave behind won't shine if those around them are better than themselves. A good leader develops better leaders than the leader leading them.

Holding back your team's ability in fear of them becoming better than you is like giving birth to a child who's hands are tied behind their back. Every now and then, I come across leaders who see a vast amount of raw talent within their teammates, and they never fully develop that person in fear that they might actually become better than the person leading the team.

And most of the time, they don't even realize they are doing this. It's a subconscious move in their leadership, simply because they feel like they have to be the best, because they are suppose to be the best.

Friend…please understand, that is not true. As a matter of fact, that couldn't be more false.

This ego that triggers leaders to control the growth in their teammates stems from a fear of not leaving a legacy; both in the present and in the future. Leaders can easily birth their ego, but it's hard for them to let it disappear. To completely develop those around you, the monster that is your ego must die.

The first problem here is that most legacies are selfish.

They are controlled by one person's achievements. A personal legacy is like a tree that doesn't bear any fruit; even though it might be a mighty oak tree, it will die with no seeds to produce a grand forest. Your legacy should be one that grows those around you for generations to come, not just your name for two years after you are dead.

Shaping leaders is a passion of mine. I'm a pastor in San Francisco, and my personal role to lead the culture of worship in our church. This means I primarily lead our worship and music teams. However, my role is not to simply lead worship; as a matter of fact, I find success when I lead less. If I am leading less, that means that I am building leaders around me that can lead better than myself.

In this chapter, we're going to take time looking at the legacy you will leave, both personal and communal. We'll focus on what we are creating, and what impact those things will have on people once we are gone, but more importantly, we're going to step away from looking at our individual artistry and focus on those makers who look to you for inspiration and mentoring.

I want to challenge you to break the mirror in front of you and see those in front of it. When you are long gone from this earth, those who you grow will invest the knowledge you have invested in them to their teammates. That is a legacy that will spread like wildfire.

To help us understand what this type of legacy means, we're going to talk about a friend of mine named Steve.

15 years ago, Steve was in a major accident. Steve was on his way home from work when he skirted off the road during a rainstorm. He braced for impact as his car collided into a electric pole off to the side of the road. After the collision, he looked around, and thought everything was normal, until he looked at his hand.

Tim had severely broken all 10 of his fingers, as well as fracturing both of his wrists.

The initial shock was more than Steve could bare. Immediately, he started telling himself "this is dream, this didn't just happen," but reality soon kicked in once the pain of the tragic accident hit his brain.

The worst part about this accident is that Steve sat there in waiting for help for almost two hours. After two hours passed, someone finally saw his car off to the side of the road and called for help.

You should also know that Steve is a piano player by trade.

As a fellow musician, He wishes he could say that towards the end of that two hour wait, he was able to come to peace with what appeared to be the end of his piano career. Steve works on major musical compositions for a living. The majority of his life was spent working on musical projects. Steve was fixated on the idea of writing "the one." For Steve, this meant the one piece that would catapult his career and discography to the world to showcase his piano abilities.

Over the period of the next 7 months, Tim was in recovery from two hand surgeries, as well as multiple therapy sessions. After a period of 13 months, his hands were healed enough to start playing piano again.

But following his recovery, Steve struggled with the implications of surviving the trauma, especially once getting back to the piano. But the trauma wasn't a physical one: it was an emotional one.

During his recovery, Steve realized what type of legacy he was pursuing, and how selfish it was. Steve was fixated on multiplying his personal platform and making himself known.

What Steve realize is that his ultimate legacy wasn't found in his piano performance, but how he could pass down his legacy to others.

Nine years later, life handed him his next big legacy lesson when he said "I do" to his wife. It wasn't until after his accident that he even considered the notion of living for anything other than himself.

And while marriage may sound like the greatest test of removing selfishness from a personal platform, Steve soon learned this was only the beginning of him sharing his legacy platform.

Three months into their marriage, Steve's wife said those two words that changes everything for any couple: "I'm pregnant."

Steve's most disruptive education in legacy began with the birth of his son in early 2004, followed by another child 22 months later. Steve told me, that "Marriage changes your worldview, but having kids injects your worldview with a serum requiring you to validate the past and future beliefs, thoughts, and actions."

Over time, Steve's legacy still grew within his piano platform, but now, he'll tell you that he cares more about his children's legacy than his own. His worldview isn't a 24-hour turnaround with his musical compositions, but the long-term vision that his children create thy what he invests into them.

"Legacy building, especially within your children is more letting them figure things out than providing answers . It's an excellent opportunity to reinforce our own convictions on everything from photosynthesis to faith," says Steve.

Case and point: the combination of Steve's shattered hands and the birth of his children made him understand why our platforms and legacies can't be selfish.

"If I die, my legacy would die with me," Steve said. "And I don't want that. I know what I invest into my children will benefit their children, and so on."

Friends: the power of living life with a legacy found in others and not yourself doesn't require kids, a spouse or a near-death experience. Instead, envision the impact of your life if every interaction was an opportunity to create a legacy. Imagine a legacy that would branch beyond your family to every person with whom you interact meaningfully enough that it leaves an imprint on them.

Because that is a legacy that has an extreme purpose.

We all reach a moment in our lives where we start searching for a purpose. A purpose that is greater than ourselves. A purpose where our life touches other lives in a meaningful way to the extent that they pass on the goodwill that they had received from us.

Here's the question you must ask yourself: as you move forward, where you do see yourself? Where would you like to "end up"? Will you create a life of value and purpose with the days you have left?

When people think of a legacy, they sometimes think about the possessions or financials they want to leave behind. However, if we all decide to live a virtuous life, a life reflecting our values and our beliefs, we can be assured that will be our destiny in life, and eventually our legacy. In the book *The Seven Habits of Highly Effective People* by Stephen Covey, the second habit mentioned is 'to always start with the end in mind'.

Once you know where you want to end up, you can start on how to get there. To begin with, the end in mind is to begin today with the image of the end of your life.

By keeping your purpose clearly in mind, you can make certain that you are reaching this goal each day of your life in a meaningful way. You need to take action. In this case, making every effort to live your values on a daily basis. What you "do" is a reflection of what you value most and your actions will speak louder than your words. A life of purpose isn't something you envision and then that's the end of it. It's something you create by taking purposeful actions. Our personal ethos is a way of being who we are and how we want others to be impacted by our actions.

What is the one thing you could start doing now that would have the most positive impact on your life and the people around you? Friends: start with that notion today. Practice your virtues daily and do it with conviction. Practice like they are rituals. Rituals become habits, and habits lead you to your destiny and your destiny is your legacy. By starting with the end in mind, you know you will get there.

It's true that we often feel our daily living interferes with the ultimate potential of our creative legacy. But, it does not have to be that way. If you know what you want to do, and how you're going to use what you do to develop your personal legacy, then you can make decisions with these goals in mind and step by step you will get there. What do you cherish? What do you think and believe? Your personal strategies include the most important talents and personal traits that you can, and will, use to accomplish your mission and get ever closer to your personal vision.

You are your own personal artwork; think about your strategies as the main values you will use to create your legacy.

It's important to choose what you do wisely. When you understand your vision, your mission, and your values, then your daily choices will lead you ever closer to your legacy. Invest in yourself now by giving yourself the gift of consistent direction to keep you on track, more fulfilled and true to your values, and living your vision. Only then will you fully be offering the world your most powerful personal legacy.

But trust me when I say, this isn't going to happen each and every day.

We all have bad days as leaders leaving a legacy. And for those of us who are fixated in leaving a legacy that invests in others, we view each day with much intention. But bad days, good days, horrible days, amazing days….they come and go. But the true, defining ones are the days that completely come at you at a surprise. And sometimes, that can be good or bad. And because we are people leaving a legacy for people, we fixate ourselves on what people say.

Which means most of those bad days start with a complaint.

As a leader in leaving a legacy, you're going to have people that just flat out don't like you.

Your personality.

Your demeanor.

Your humor. (I get this one a lot, mainly from my wife)

Your character.

That's a hard thing to take in – not the fact that someone doesn't like what you do, but that they don't like you. And yeah, it hurts. But here's the great thing about it. Complaints are always a way to make you stronger. Whether they were meant to refine you, or simply meant to hurt you – take it, learn from it, and make it part of the structure of your leadership.

As a leader, you have to decide a few things:

Am I going to take it personally, or am I going to learn from it? That's your first step. If we were honest, it's hard not to take criticism personally if it's coming from someone with a judgmental attitude. However, you can do what you should do:

Love them, regardless of their selfish opinions,

…or you could:

Stay mad at them for an extended period of time, with no reconciliation or true Biblical forgiveness.

Remember…it's on them. Don't take it personally. Always evaluate what you did, and if you simply come to the conclusion that it was simply an "I don't like you" spirit…then forgive, and move on. This points back to what we discussed in the last chapter about having authentic artistry. Your legacy is a masterpiece, and as long as you are authentic in the design of it, you won't have anything to apologize for.

And trust me when I say, you have more important things to do than to dwell on this issue.

As Shannon Alder said, *"Carve your name on hearts, not tombstones. A legacy is etched into the minds of others and the stories they share about you."* [7]

"On the most fundamental of levels we were born to create," says Liz, who is a writer, artist, and filmmaker. "Every moment of our lives is being shaped by our intention, thoughts, actions and behaviors. Everyone is a creator, but not everyone is an artist. I like to think of artists as Extra Intentional Creators, those that consciously take nothing and turn it into something."

I remember sitting down and talking to Liz about legacy. And the weirdest thing happened during our talk.

She started telling me how she's obsessed with death.

So, I asked her the most basic question after her comment about death.

"Donnie Darko is like, your all time favorite movie then?"

"I hated every minute of it," said Liz.

Donnie Darko is in my top five, by the way.

I was really intrigued why she thought on death so much. I've known Liz for quite some time, and she's someone who enjoys life to its fullest.

"Keeping death in mind reminds me of these false beliefs that my life is mine and ONLY mine to live. This helps me to live better."

What I've learned from Liz is this: death can easily ask us, "what parts of me will stick around after I am gone?"

I'm a multi-passionate person. I know the ups and downs of having an interest in various mediums, genres, and processes. I've spent too many days finding something new and exciting and investing my entire being into a project that replicates what I just found.

This juggling can be important to early stages of creation. To produce a legacy that can be passed down generation to generation, we may need to remove things from our lives. Not just on removing the day-to-day distractions that prevents us from fully expressing ourselves, but also on creating one thing at a time. Paint when you are painting, write when you are writing, and so forth.

Liz taught me about meditating on the idea that leaving a legacy narrows down to two specific things: focus and voice. If we want to leave a lasting legacy, one that will continue to speak after we're gone, we need to tap into these two aspects of our creative process.

To constantly toggle back and forth between things is to do a disservice to your work. It stretches your focus, waters down your intent, and interrupts the flow of your process. With focused spurts of time, we can truly get deep and bring forth a complete expression.

And then, there is voice.

Honing one's voice takes time. For every idea, there is something that wants to be expressed. It's our job to determine the medium of this expression, as well as how it will be "said." Honing your voice is not about one project; it's about multiple projects, months of projects, years of projects. Voice is about the unique fingerprint you bring to the expression. Since every one of us is unique in our history, experiences, and point of view, our voices are unique too. It takes an incredibly diligent creator to ignore the voice of others and reveal their own voice, but this is what's required when building a legacy.

After having this discussion with Liz, she asked, "How will you bring focus to your days, weeks, months and years in order to fulfill that legacy? What steps have you taken to uncover your own unique voice that will resonate through time? What will your creative legacy be?"

I thought on this for a while, and while meditating on this aspect for a couple minutes, my answer was simple: "People. My creative legacy will be found in people."

Liz responded, "Your creative legacy will never be found in people. Because if you invest your creative legacy inside of people, your legacy will always be transparent; because what they create may have your foundation to their work, but you as a person will be nonexistent. You'll be invisible."

I said, "I feel like that's how it should be. I don't want copycats of me. I want people to take what I know and make it their own."

Liz said, "Exactly. And THAT is how you build the greatest personal legacy." [8]

Your ceiling is the next generation's floor.

Build well.

CHAPTER FIVE:
Tooth and Nail

People would label me a "creative." And we either hate or love how we work.

It's one of the things that the creative types tend to hate. We all have that specific time of day when the individual genius of who we are starts to pour out of our heads and onto our tools of trade. We get into a series of daily space where we know exactly what works for us, what time of day works best, and what things makes us produce art of better quality.

In this chapter, were going to focus on a foundational tool of creativity, leadership, legacy and success: hard work.

Yes. I said the two words most artists hate.

Hard. Work.

I was born in raised in an environment where hard work was not only required, but valued. Growing up in the rural midwest, I quickly learned the value of "not getting above your raising." This term was thrown around like hotcakes (the term "thrown around like hotcakes" was also thrown around quite a bit as well), and I quickly understood that seeing progression meant working hard at it.

I firmly believe that at its core, hard work is a ritual that each artist, leader, and creative must have to see their dreams become a reality.

A ritual. Not a routine. Because I don't believe in routines.

Sidebar time. Routines are stupid. They're wrong. They make me want to take a piece of paper, write the word "routine" on it, and light it on fire.

In case you missed it, let me say again, I don't believe in routines.

Rituals, however, that's a whole other story.

I'm extremely ritualistic. I believe that rituals are what make me tick.

Before we go any further, let me explain what a ritual is to me. It's the driving force of a daily agenda where I pour all that I am into that segment of the day. My work schedule. My workout. The times of day when I get to speak love to my people. My time secluded and alone. My creative moments where something sparks inside my head.

Check out what how Webster's dictionary explains the two:

Routine: *a fixed program / performed for a regular procedure, rather than a special reason.*

Ritual: *a ceremony consisting of special actions to perform a specific task.*

I don't know about you, but I don't want a routine. I don't want to be "fixed into a program." I don't want to perform "regular procedure." I want everything in my life to be an action where it brings me to perform a relevant task in my life.

Let me stop you right there. Because at this point, you're already thinking "but I have to do *this* or *that* no matter what, whether I like it or not."

Friend: what would it look like if you made every single thing that you do relevant to who you are? Have ownership over it. Make it as great as can be. And you'll soon find out that your routines will become slaves to your rituals.

You don't want mediocre day to day. You want passionate moments by moments.

I think it's time we all sit-down and revaluate our daily routines, and slowly figure out if what we are doing is just because we have to do it, or it's because it means something to us and to those we love.

Here's what I want to challenge you with today: dive into the unknown. Own your daily schedule. Start getting ritualistic, and dump the routine. By doing this, you'll see excellence in almost every area of your life. It's not something brought about overnight, but it can be achieved.

Here's the flip side: your friends probably won't do this. Why? Simply because it takes of a lot of hard work. The one thing that most makers forget is that consistency in itself is hard work. And when you combine hard work with consistency, excellence is your bi-product.

Too often, makers become so satiated in their current state of artistry that the fuse for change tends to fizzle out. We look around our artistic platform and realize things look nice, updated, and refreshing, so we stay that way for months, or in some cases years at a time. It seems as if artists can become very complacent in their calling (and sometimes their paycheck) so they tend to stop pushing the artistic button.

On the flip side, you have those makers who want to push the button, but they have no clue where to start. And sometimes, they are even afraid of change.

For the next few paragraphs, we're going to outline some ways you can make your artistry go from "eh" to excellent.

Say the same thing, but in a different way.

If we look at scripture, we constantly see Jesus presenting His message in very different and illustrated ways. This is my greatest example of using my platform for an artist message. Presenting your artwork in a new exciting way can help you leak out the gospel to people who typically would not recognize it. Spread the same message you always have, but be looking for different ways you can express it.

Make everything absolutely beautiful.

The brushes. The stained glass. The stage. Your website. Every. Single. Inch. I can't express this enough: from the moment your artwork is visible to the public, it is your privilege to make every inch of your art a presentation of the message that is inside of you. Whatever it is, it's your job to make everything look absolutely flawless.

Push the button and make them leave their comfort zone.

Try something completely off the wall. Branch out for ideas and expressions that you don't think you can do, and then try your best to make them work until you have been able to see it accomplished.

You must be able to speak the same artistry as your people, but make sure that your art and focus are not presented in the same way all the time. Bounce ideas off of other people; read creativity blogs, and then try to present something that will give your people the "shock and awe" factor.

I talked about these ideas with a friend of mine named Donald. We're going to call him Don for short. Don was stuck in a rut of seeing nothing getting accomplished each day of his work week.

When I first asked Don about his work schedule, he said, "Seriously man, I just try to let the work flow and see what happens."

Don is a local artist in Las Vegas who paints murals on buildings for a living. He had reached out to me for help, because he was losing clientele, losing his family, and not seeing any growth in his company, or himself.

My first question to Don was: "How many hours a week do you work?"

His response: "At the minimum, 50."

Don was working for 50 hours a week, and he was seeing nothing come out of it. Could you imagine that type of feeling Don was feeling?

I recently read an article that in the United States, we work more per hour and per week than any other developed nation. In the high-paced social and corporate ladder that is our current nation, it is so easy for us to lose a sense of rest. We are all trying to achieve. We are all trying to dominate. We are all trying to climb.

When in all reality, all we are really end up doing is staying afloat. So the first thing Don and I worked on is his rest.

"Seriously, dude? The first step towards more clients is rest?" I don't believe a second of it."

I quickly learned that if Don was to continue his current pace of work, he'd eventually fizzle out and stop work completely, with not income or clients. So, I taught Don about Shalom.

Shalom is a Hebrew word that simply means "peace". It's a term used among Jews to give peace to one another. Just saying the word brings peace to my spirit. It's a beautiful, restful word. One God has given us to bring peace upon our current status quo.

Every now and then, we all need Shalom. And Don definitely needed it. Don and I talked about three ways he could find Shalom in his work:

1. Stop.
Stop what you are doing. Right now. It's not that important. Your family is more important than that thing. Your health is better off without that overtime at work. Your relationships will succeed because you stopped.

2. Breathe.
Take a big deep breath of air. Relax. Give yourself some slack. Run your hands through your hair, and sit back. Look around, cherish that beauty that is around you, and be happy.

3. Maintain.
Stop trying to climb the latter. No reason to you have to do it now. Just rest.

It's really that simple. Everyone needs those moments.
Truth be told, it's these moments that help me charge the
gates of everyday pressures....those moments when God
whispers "Don't worry, I got this. You just sit back and
rest."

I talked about this aspect of rest with Don. The one thing
he kept mentioning was "But what if if see succession,
but I'm not happy with it? I could never go back to the
way I'm working now, which scares me, because I
actually like working 50 hours a week.

Here's what I realized about Don: he was a hard worker.
But he was obsessed with working hard. He was
addicted to work, and because of that, he couldn't see
that this was hurting his career, but more importantly, his
life.

Don was stuck in a place where he felt like as a person
he as succeeding because he was putting in the hours,
but his paycheck was telling him something else. He
was stuck in a place where he couldn't see the end game
anymore because he felt like he had to work these hours
to accomplish something.

You see, Don was getting satisfaction from wearing himself out. Here's the problem with that: this was doing absolutely nothing for his career, and he was killing his relationships around him because of his work. It was very selfish, and was doing nothing but giving him a tired body with no positive outcome.

Don and I went on a very long, tedious journey to help him work hard, but in a smart way.

It took months.

And a lot of blood, sweat and tears.

No, really. Blood. He got a nose bleed once during one of our meetings.

For the rest of this chapter, I'm going to outline the journey Don and I went on.

1. Don stoped returning to what hadn't worked.
Whether a job or a broken relationship that was ended for a good reason, we should never go back to the same thing, expecting different results, without something being different.

2. Don stopped doing anything that required him to be someone he wasn't.

In everything we do, we have to ask ourselves, "Why am I doing this?" Am I suited for it? Does it fit me? Is it sustainable?"

3. Don stopped believing he could please everyone.

This is one I think all of us deal with at some point. It's impossible to please everyone. Once you understand this, you begin to live purposefully, trying to please the right people.

5. Don reminded himself that his inner life determines his outer success.

Everyone makes mistakes, even the most successful people out there. But, what achievers do better than others is recognize the patterns that are causing those mistakes and never repeat them again. In short, they learn from pain—their own and the pain of others.

A good thing to remember is this: pain is unavoidable, but repeating the same pain twice, when we could choose to learn and do something different, is certainly avoidable.

6. Don worked less.

People tend to be productive for 4.5 hours a day, but many of us have to stretch it to 8 or 9. As a result, our minds invent distractions as a way out, and also as a way to seem productive even when we're not. That's when you start browsing the web, emailing, texting, tweeting and seeing what everyone is up to on Facebook.

7. Don had a daily quota.

Don committed to just one client every day. He used a spreadsheet to log his work hours for that one client. What we saw was that Don's work began to increase, but a particular client saw that Don spent an entire day with him, and that client could tell he really cared for him.

8. Don front-loaded his creative process.

Don started his work at 6 a.m. This game him a sprint into his day, and then by the afternoon, he didn't feel like he was playing catch up.

9. Don learned to multitask.

It helped Don to embrace his scattered brain and sometime do two things at once. I'd he would paint one thing, then go make coffee, and while making coffee, Don would think of something I wanted to add to my art project. Taking a "coffee break" was actually Don's way to getting out of his art box and thinking more creatively.

10. Don remove his distractions.

When distractions reach a boiling point, Don would take drastic measures. There was even one point where he ended putting all of his electronic devices in a box in his car during the work day to make sure he could stay focuses on his work.

11. But Don also made distractions intentional.

Don realized that distractions invite the mind to wander and the body to move, so we started to let them happen. And even sometimes they would spark new thought patterns and creative collisions.

These 11 steps helped Don tremendously with his career. But there was one major problem that underlined the entire system of our 11 steps.

And I have a feeling you also deal with this as well.

The work/life balance.

For me personally, the work/life balance is a messy one. But here's something that could be a problem for you as it was for Don: the fact that we call it work/life balance automatically implies that one of the two is negative.

While one should be above the other, we have to learn that it's *balance* with the other.

Work/life is not either/or, it's both/and. It's a life we all live every day. In this regard, we can't look at work and life as separate. They are the same, there is only one thing, it's called LIFE. Work is part of my life, it's not competing against it. Family is important, friends are important but it's not competing against my work.

My work is a huge part of who I am as a person. I believe work is one of the most important things in one's life. I believe that work is on of the reasons I get up in the morning. It's what I love to do with most of my days.

I strongly believe that every person can make a living doing something they love. And often enough, it's more of a mindset to become happy with your work. Often it's not the work that sucks, but how we see it. Ultimately, it's only "work" if you don't like it. If you love doing what you do, it doesn't feel like work. And yes, you still need balance, because you need balance with everything you do.

But what you don't need is life/work balance, because if you do, you might need to make some drastic changes with either one of them. And this either means changing your job or simply looking at your job from a different perspective.

I mean, just look at how much society celebrates Fridays and hates Mondays. Shouldn't it be the other way around? Imagine a world where we all loved what we do so much that we would be all sad every Friday because it would take us away from something we love doing.

I'm not saying there is something wrong with taking a break from any activity, but just the way we as society "hate" Mondays is what's so surprising to me. If I could decide, on Mondays we should all celebrate because the world is awake again. As makers, we can put in the work, get some stuff done and do what we love.

But what if we even took it a step further? What if we celebrated the Mondays AND the Fridays?

Work and life is a balance. Your life outside of work is just as important as your work. Celebrate both.

After working with Don on his work/life balance, I decided I needed to do the same and take a look at my own balance of life.

At a young age I was told, "Without hard work, nothing grows but weeds."

I was also told, "With hard work, it was possible to achieve the American Dream."

I wasn't sure what the American Dream was because growing up in the rural midwest America, my thought of the American Dream was a family, a big house, and a career with job security.

Basically, my opinion of the American Dream was stability.

The world looked incredible to me growing up, and I was passionate about waking up every day and exploring. I wondered why my the typical midwesterner around me didn't seem to be passionately alive.

It was because status-quo became survival to them. Their everyday eventual turned into "the need for the paycheck," which then diluted their passion down to be non-existent.

Makers: living the American Dream can easily feel like living the American Nightmare. Working hard is a suitable tool for a maker, but working hard can also be a monster.

As a maker, we must act from acting from passions more than our hard work.

You may have some thoughts about the conflict of working hard vs. acting from passion. I know I did. If you're not doing hard work, you may feel lazy or guilty. Or like it's too good to be true. Following your passion seems like it's easy, yet it can be hard work too. But it's the kind of hard that's fueled by pleasure and passion.

This begs the question, "how do you begin acting from your passions?"

Put passion first, even if it's only in your thoughts at first.

When you want to discover and act from your passion, you may have thoughts that challenge this new way of letting go of "hard" and gliding into joy and passion.

Accept how hard your work and life really are and must be for now.

Know that sometimes life is hard. And work is hard. World and life events and tragedies bring us down out of happiness and passion. Know that this is necessary so you can see the contrast of living from passion first to living from the work hard place.

Remember, when you have passion about something, you are more willing to take risks. Everyone can decide to work hard, but passion means something different to each person. Follow yours.

You can have one leader that leads with hard work and another that leads with passion. Which one do you want to follow?

Ask yourself some tough questions,

What do you feel passionate about?

If you have no idea, remember what you loved doing as a kid. What were your favorite toys and games?

What activities do you partake in that, when you do them, you lose all sense of time?

What do you really want to do but are afraid to say out loud?

Close your eyes while contemplating this question. Feel the answers in your heart instead of thinking them with your head.

Passion is not always strong and powerful. It can be calm and deep. Don't worry about motivation. Once you feel the passion for something, the motivation comes with little effort.

Put passion before hard work, but don't forget hard work is needed to make your passions come alive.

And that's what Don did. And now, Don is making a much larger salary, doesn't have too much stress.

Whenever I want to talk to him about his work, he always says, "sure, but I gotta tell you this story about my kids real quick."

CHAPTER SIX:
Dreamers and Thinkers

One day during art class, my teacher walked by my desk as we were making snowmen out of cotton balls. *10

Yes, this is the same project I said was extremely boring in chapter two.

At the time, I was completely fixated on this adventure I had dreamt up in my head about a rodent who owned his own 2-story house. The story was called *"Mouse in a House,"* and it was a 6-page fully illustrated novel (on construction paper) about…you guessed it…a mouse in a house.

I was totally not doing the snowman project and was totally daydreaming about the book I wanted to make.

She walked by my desk and said, "Did I just catch you daydreaming?"

I looked at her and said, "did it look like I was daydreaming?"

She replied, "yes."

I said, "okay."

We had this weird 5-second stare down contest where I thought she was either going to throw me into detention or out the window - but she moved on to the next desk, praising the girl behind on how colorful her snowman was.

Cool story, huh?

Yeah I thought so too.

This story holds no real value outside of two facts:
1. My art teacher hated me.
2. I firmly believe in the art of storytelling.

We spend a lot of time finding the right words. We look for words that will differentiate us from everyone around us. We want to be able to tell our story in the most authentic and passionate way. And even though we've assembled the perfect words, there can still be a disconnect from your mouth to people's minds.

When you ready a story that feels inauthentic, it's usually not because the storyteller didn't find the right words. It's because they weren't clear about their intention. In return, their message becomes jumbled and confusing. We can't expect to speak and act in alignment with our values if we haven't agreed on what those values are, why they matter and how they will manifest.

Storytellers: here's the depressing side of all of this:

In the last 60 seconds that it took you to read that last paragraph, 168 million emails were sent, 700,000 Google searches were launched, and 60 hours of YouTube videos were uploaded. Thousands of spam emails were opened, and millions of Facebook posts, tweets, texts, and telemarketing calls found their way to someones doorstep.

Here's something even more crazy.

A whopping 90% of all data in the world has been generated in the past two years alone.

90. Percent.

Talk about information overload.

If you are committed to delivering a meaningful, memorable message to another human being, the burning question you need to be asking is this: "How can I cut through all of the background noise so my message can be heard and remembered?"

Fear not, teller of stories.

Storytelling is the most effective, time-tested way to transmit meaning from one human being to another. It's how civilizations pass on their wisdom to the next generation. It's how religions pass on the sacred teachings of faith. And through fables and fairy tales, it's the way all of us has been transmitted the values from our parents.

But there's a core truth to storytelling and why it captivates us all in a certain way. Storytelling enables trust and connection between the speaker and listener. Why is this? when you hear a story, in any way, your brain starts to try to connect yourself to the story. And almost every time, your brain will knit itself to the story in some degree.

My favorite thing about storytelling is this: it translates values. It helps people make sense out of the world. It reframes frustration and depravity. It lets us shake hands with our suffering, because we our reality is being retold through a meaningful message.

In this chapter, we're going to meditate on one of the most, if not the most powerful tool of a maker; Story.

Fish aren't taught to swim. The sun wasn't taught to set. And you were not taught to tell stories. As a child, you didn't need to be taught.

Storytelling is instinctual.

It's just there. Like learning how to walk. To eat. To blink. It's in your bones and has been since you were very young.

At this point, you may be thinking "I don't tell stories." I would debate that. Because telling stories isn't just something you do verbally.

You tell stories through your actions.

You tell stories through your parenting.

Your tell stories through your legacy.

You tell stories because you are maker.

You tell stories because of your monsters.

Friend: no matter what you do, simply just by living your life, you are telling a story.

You are telling *your* story.

And everyone likes a good story.

Your story is one worth sharing. But while your life may be your story, there's a good and bad way to tell it. We all want to be a *good* storyteller and we all want to tell stories that captivate people.

For a good period of time, I was obsessed with M. Night Shyamalan's works. So much so that when I was in high school, I had to write a paper on a fictional character, so I made up a fictional character called N. Day Shabaloo that was the alter-ego of M. Night Shyamalan.

And while 87% of you disagree with me (I guessed on the percentage, but from talks with friends, I can't be that far off), I personally think his work is genius.

Hey M. Night…sorry for what I'm about to say. Love you, dude.

I get it. Some of his plot lines are really corny. And *The Last Airbender* was…I don't even know. And yeah, *The Village* was great until 10 minutes into it when you figured out the entire story. And *Signs* was awesome, outside of, you know, Mel Gibson.

I really hope M. Night never reads this book. I'll deny all of this.

But when I think of a good story, I think of the movie *Lady in the Water.* In my opinion that was his best work outside of *The Sixth Sense* that just cannot be touched with a 10 foot Siskel & Ebert pole.

Lady in the Water was a folklore in the present tense. From beginning to end, cinematography to plot, it was genius.

And while I love his work (well, most of it *cough Mel Gibson cough*), I don't want to be M. Night Shyamalan.

Because being yourself is one of the secrets to being a good storyteller.

First, to tell your authentic, powerful story, you have to stop telling yourself the story that you don't know how to tell a good story.

And then, you have to tell *your* story.

Communicating your humanity is an artwork in the most simplistic sense. The more human you are willing to be, the more likely it is that people will connect with your story.

Everyone wants something to hold on to. And when you are sharing your story, by being authentic to its structure, you are simply respecting your audience.

So, storyteller, are you ready to learn how to tell your story in the most impactful way? Let's put some tangible actions in place to make this happen.

The science of telling a good story is much less complicated that you think. Fundamentally, it's all about structure and the inter-relationships of the elements that comprise the structure. Just like a house needs a foundation, a story needs structure, too. And once you understand the elements of story structure, you're halfway home.

I remember a friend of mine named Alex who threw everything to the curb and moved to Greenland to work on a fishing boat for six months just to get away from it all. Sounds like a fun story, right?

Once Alex's six months were up, we talked about his time out on the sea:

"It was fun, man. Lots of cool stuff happened. Overall, it was a pretty cool experience."

"Dude...like, that's all you have to say?"

Listen I get it. Some of us are quieter than most. Alex and I share that bond with each other. I'm not one to immediately become vibrant with my words once asked about my day. As a matter of fact, you'd more than likely get a response that is something like, "well, it hasn't sucked."

Storytelling is suppose to be authentic people. Don't judge me.

Aside from lacking a certain oomph, the story about being out on the sea, as Alex told it, made him come off as a bit bland.. But I had this weird feeling Alex's story didn't reflect who he truly was, so I asked Alex:

"Can you describe the moment you knew you were living your personal dream by being out there on the sea?"

That's when Alex told me about the day he was out on the water, with no bank account, no cell phone, no bills, and nothing but the cans of spam in the galley and the two shirts he was wearing.

"It was the most freeing feeling in the world, man. It's how I knew I was suppose to be here, doing that at that exact time."

After Alex told me that, I said, "I feel like I can trust you more. You're not someone who's afraid to change course when things truly aren't working, not someone who just gave up. I can't explain it, but I feel like you're more creative now."

In order for your story to work its magic on an audience, you have to structure it properly. We're going to take a moment to dissect why I connected to Alex's story.

When you tell your story, tell stories as scenes, not as summaries.

When you're telling a story, you're constantly making a choice between the two narrative modes that writers call scene and summary.

"I took my worn jacket out of my the closet, snapped it together, and walked onto the bridge of the cold boat stained with seaweed and sea water" is scene.

"I put on my jacket," is summary.

Stories connect better with audiences when you convey your inciting incident as a scene. Especially when the incident involves suffering, failure, disillusionment or struggle on your part.

As both Alex and I learned, everyone you talk to will feel more connected to the people in your stories if you use scene instead of summary.

So, maker: tell more stories. Use scene. People will learn to trust you. Because you are more like everyone else than you think.

Within any aspect of a maker, I firmly believe there are leadership qualities that exist. And while that may not be for a platform stance, your artistry has a message attached to its core, which means you a leading people to a certain thought pattern. [11]

But sometimes as a creative, our workflow will get in the way of storytelling.

Typically, my schedule when I enter a coffee shop goes something like this:

open door - get in line - order coffee - find a dark, quiet corner to work in - make no eye contact with anyone - stay completely unsociable - work - read - work - contemplate - think - leave.

However, three weeks ago while wrapping up the "leave" section of my coffee shop agenda, I did something completely irrational. Something so over-the-top, unthinkable, and highly unattainable for someone of my introverted status.

I started a conversation with a complete stranger.

I remember starting the walk to my car when I notice a middle-aged man opening a small wooden box containing pieces stained glass in the form of a dream catcher. It caught my attention, more than most things of this nature would.

I walked right past him, headed to complete the rest of my typical unsociable day when my mind stopped me and said "nope. you gotta do it. Otherwise, it'll bother you all night."

I turned around, look at this complete strange and muddled out some words such as "Sorry to bother you. I know this is super weird. But for some reason, I'm extremely curious about these things in this box of yours."

Now typically, someone who is writing out this story now begins to tell you how this conversation was about his grandmother who was an immigrant who made a living in downtown NYC during the 1950's by making these trinkets and started a legacy for her family and then this guy being her grandson now runs his multi-million dollar company by selling these dreamcatchers and blah blah blah. And then I'm supposed to tell you that this is what networking and connecting with strangers is all about, so you can be inspired.

Well, that didn't happen.

It was just some guy. Just a normal guy, with a box of hand-me-downs his mother gave him. He picked a sunny day to sit outside of a coffee shop and investigate this box of stained glass dreamcatchers. He told me a little bit about his family, his heritage, and how his mother's things were willed to him. And that was it.

I thanked him for his time and moved on with my day of complete unsociability.

Here's where all of this starts to make sense.

Situations like these – conversations that bring change of pace, is what makes up new, provocative, innovated stories.

I pondered on this guy all day long after meeting him. I thought about how I didn't know him from Adam. I wondered what else he would find in this box. I contemplated if he would come across something that would completely change his course of life.

And it made me smile. Because it showed me that when I mix up the things I typically would do in my life, it makes me grow in places I didn't think I needed to grow in.

If I'm saying anything at all, I'm saying this – do something today that is completely outside of YOU, because that's how great stories are created. Do something you would never do. These occurrences in our lives that we tend to keep locked away in the depth of who we are can actually destroy our creativity. Branch out today. Shake someone's hand you weren't expecting to shake. Blend up your schedule and do something completely irrational.

But there is a balance to this. the flip side of this coin is when you do something so completely outside of you that you end up shadowing the authentic portion of your artistry.

"Think outside the box. ALWAYS think outside the box." That's what almost every single creative person I know has told me. And if I were honest, it's done me more harm than good. For a long time in my ministry career, my job dictated me created a Sunday morning experience that combined artwork, music, technically and anything you could possibly imagine to create a fantastic Sunday experience. And while I directed these multiple moving art pieces each week, I was constantly reminded of one thing: this world of artistry is always changing.

Therefore, we seem to think we have to change. Which means new, fresh, exciting ideas. Right? I mean, isn't that always the answer?

Fortunately for us, it isn't.

It was mid-August, and I found myself preparing for our Christmas Eve service. This was THE service. the one where hundreds of people would come to our church to see a full-blown-production-driven concert about Jesus and Christmas. On a Saturday morning, I sat in a room with the 7 people who were helping me create this experience, looked at them and said: "I'm on a creative plateau. I have no new ideas. What I do have, is 12 unfinished projects I am currently working on. And I've decided to put them all on hold."

They all seriously looked like they wanted to kill me.

Here's the reason why: I'm not producing excellent, polished projects. I'm thinking too much. I'm doing too much. And the stuff I am producing is in my opinion, a little less than mediocre.

As a maker, there are three different things you can do to make your old, dusty ideas into solid gold.

Stop dumbing down your ideas. Pick one idea you've had in the past…maybe even one that you have accomplished. Make it better. Maximize, maximize, maximize. Your ideas start out as an oasis in a desert-and by the time you unleash this new project, it's already part of the desert. Add more water. Plant more seeds. Grow your oasis into a tropical island, and then invite everyone to it.

Stop trading effectiveness for busyness. New project. New idea. New brainstorming session. New. New. New. In a society that is always moving, always working, and never ending, creative artists often feel like they have to live up to this status quo. Such is not the case. Work slow, work hard, work smart, and do not unleash your project until it's the best work you've ever done.

Never leave your culture box. I have this thing I call a "culture box." It's the box where my church body lives – what they see as relevant, what they worship to, and what they consider effective. It's the language of presentation that they actually hear…and I have to speak to that – otherwise, they won't listen. When it comes to our new ideas, make sure your creative box is limited to the culture that you sending the message to. Otherwise, they won't even listen.

New ideas are never bad. As a matter of fact, they are healthy. But you don't have to do them all right now. Cherish the projects that you have open, even if you are losing momentum or gusto. Select wisely, move forward with relevance, and unleash the project with confidence.

There's two different types of creatives: the producers and the inventors. The producers are people who are constantly coming up with ideas and figuring out a way to make all of them come to life. The inventors are people who have a strike of genius and spend quite a bit of time on one project, and eventually release something absolutely mind-blowing.

For this particular Christmas Eve service, I needed to take the roll as a producer, which meant my flow looks something like this: new story = new project = new task. Which then equals more work flow. Tons, and tons, and tons of work flow. And that's why I was stagnant in my ideas for our experience.

You might be one of those producers who has an issue with thinking you have to deliver on every idea you bring to the table. I'm here to give you some grace; you don't have to. And to be honest, it's probably better that you don't.

1. Don't do it all at the same time. I have a big black board in my office that I write down every idea on. However, when I get to my office the next day, for some reason, I think every one of these projects needs to be done. And in return, my daily duties take a risk and becoming uncompleted tasks because I'm stressing over 6 new ideas that shouldn't even be real projects yet. The big lesson to learn here: don't spend time doing things that are going to hurt your work flow.

2. Keep your stress level low by doing one big project at a time. So after I look at my giant black board full of great ideas, those ideas start dwindling and dwindling, until they become less than mediocre work. And when it's time to showcase them, the people that I have been talking this idea up to look at me as if I haven't delivered anything at all. In all reality, it probably would have been better if I had done just that. Make sure your work flow schedule is down – add 1 project at a time. Deliver, and move on.

Remember that Christmas Eve service we were talking about earlier? We waited until October to work on it, and it ended up being the most artist experience we created to date. Think inside the box. Your culture will appreciate it.

Maker of Stories, please know that you're not alone. We got your back. But maybe it's time to wipe away all those ideas, take a breather, and pick just one for now. Always remember, storytelling is your greatest asset when utilizing your leadership platform to send a message to a group of people. Whether that's in a book, a graphic design, a song, or even something simple as an Instagram post, using stories is a surefire way to get your message into the heart of your listeners.

CHAPTER SEVEN:
Bow and Blood

What does a perfectionist do when they realize perfection is an illusion?

They give up.

There are days where I feel like I fail at every single thing that I do. And what I've come to realize is that most makers feel this same way at least once a week, if not once a day.

I've had countless talks with numerous makers about this journey to find perfectionism in our work. And when we don't reach perfectionism, we feel like our work becomes invalid.

What I've realized is this: I'm not really failing. I've just set my personal standard way to high. We've been taught perfectionism makes us better. It means we value quality work. It means we pay attention to the details. It means we hold ourselves to a higher standard. But perfectionism also kills creativity and productivity.

A perfectionist holds him or herself to unrealistic expectations, and in return, they are never satisfied with their work. They never deliver, because they never feel like their work is finished.

The funny thing is, that statement in itself is already questionable because nothing is ever finished anyways. We end up overthinking our work so much, that the work actually suffers instead of improving.

And honestly, I've learned recently that when I live a life of perfectionism, I'm sad, drained, and I never seem to be able to be satisfied.

Personally, I have spent so much time and effort wasting in perfecting my projects that it has actually kept me from getting my important work done.

I remember when my wife and I moved into our first house together. It sat on an acre lot of beautiful green grass.

But it wasn't green enough for me.

I spent countless hours researching on how to get greener grass and how often to mow your lawn. I spent hundreds of dollars spent to maintain the already semi-beautiful lawn.

All because the grass wasn't green enough.

And after 6 months, I finally got our lawn to be greener.

And no one, including my wife, even noticed or cared that the lawn was more green.

I was left with a beautiful lawn that was being showcased only to myself for no reason than to please my own sanity. Here's the kicker: two weeks later, we ended up have a serious mole problem that completely trashed the lawn. And my once "perfected" yard was now a hole-ridden dirt pile.

Have you ever been here before? Maybe some of you are like this with your coffee (me too) or your spreadsheets (me too) or your workouts (me too).

If so, then we need to start guarding ourselves from our perfectionism.

And needless to say, I'm with you there too.

First, we need to think like a child.
A child doesn't question their ideas or wonder what people think of them. They just do what they want to do. Sometimes there are consequences, but I'd rather face the consequence of failing than never try.

In 20 years, I will regret the things I didn't do way more than the things I did. By keeping our projects stupid, we keep them simple. We remove the pressure and allow ourselves the freedom to do what we want to do.

Second, we have to be okay when we produce mediocre projects.
We can we linger over a project for way to long. We can overthink every project we are working on. And this causes multiple cases of anxiety to our workload because we haven't accomplished anything that matters.

We also have to be okay when our projects suck.
Sometimes, we just miss the target completely. We shoot for the stars and land flat on our face. And when this happens, we take it personal.

Have you ever noticed that when you are working on a project and it fails, you take it personally?

"This (fill in the blank) failed, therefore, I am a failure."

Have you ever told yourself that before?

I know I have.

Maker, you cannot justify your existence based on your products. Learn to be okay when you don't reach the level of genius.

Also, we have to be okay when are projects are just "good."
Every failure is a step towards success. But every completed project that we finish doesn't have to be polished.

A perfectionist that thinks this way will find rest. Doing this doesn't mean you aren't considering the details and the quality, its acknowledging that "great" does not equal "perfect."

Saying "it's good enough" doesn't mean we are lowering our standards. We can still create something that people love. And we can usually go back and make changes later. "Good enough" simply means we are taking ownership for our projects instead of letting them own us. [12]

The perfectionist in you is resisting this advice right now, isn't he?

Being a perfectionist myself, I can read these last few pages, and think to myself "well that sounds great, but there is no way I can do these things." It's not that I think I can't do these things, it's more than I don't want to do them.

Perfectionism almost feels like a moral conviction that you cannot betray. Friends: as soon as you release yourself from perfectionism, I promise you will find yourself more creative, more productive and happier.

And trust me, that doesn't mean chasing perfectionism is completely bad. But if it's the reason you start or finish anything, the tips above might help you.

Here is something else I've learned about perfectionism: battling this monster can become toxic. The inner fight to conquer our perfectionism turns into us removing the authenticity from our lives. That happens because deep down, we feel unqualified to create what we're currently making.

Do you ever feel like a fraud? Like you've fooled everyone into thinking you know what you're doing, but you're actually completely unqualified? Do you ever feel guilty you're getting paid for the stuff you're putting out into the world?

I'll go ahead and answer this for both you and I: Yes.

Long answer: Strangely enough, the more praise we receive and the bigger platform our creations get, the more we have this feeling. It's more pressure and higher expectations we may not be able to meet. I could receive 100 compliments, but if I hear one person say, "You don't deserve this," that's the person I choose to believe.

This monsters name is called the "Imposter Syndrome." It is something that affects most of us. It affects us on different levels and it's an issue we all deal with.

The imposter syndrome scales depending on where you are in your career. In the beginning, your self-confidence might be very low, so feeling like a fraud is fairly easy because you have very little experience to back up your feelings. I felt like a fraud the moment I started out as a maker, but I thought it might disappear once I got more experience.

But the problem is, the more "successful" you become, the more it makes you feel like a fraud. The stakes become higher, more people are looking at you and you will be surrounded by people who simply don't like seeing you being successful. The more "successful" you get, the harder it will be because all eyes are now on you, and people are just waiting for you to fall and call you a fraud.

You may be suffering from what is known as the Imposter Syndrome.

And that's a pretty bad thing.

On the upside, the fact that so many people talk about feeling like a fraud makes me feel it less.

Weird, right?

Maybe we're all just really good at faking it.
Either way, we're in it together. I've given this subject a lot of thought (judging by a number of self-help books on Amazon about it) and I've found a few ways to ease this debilitating feeling.

And just a heads up, this next portion might feel like a slap in the face.

Sometimes, we have to put on our boxing gloves and beat the crap out of our monsters.

First of all, own it.
I've read a lot about the imposter syndrome and how it might hold you back. The problem is, most people see themselves as a victim of the Imposter Syndrome and render themselves useless. Some even try to get rid of it, treating it like a sickness that can be cured. The one thing I learned is that the imposter syndrome is here to stay and if I make it part of myself, it can't stop me anymore.

Here's the solution to Imposter Syndrome: the solution is to just OWN IT.

The more you work, the more you improve your skill. When you're wondering if your work is as good as someone else's, you are wasting time you could spend on getting even better. It's okay to feel like a fraud; we all will at some point. Keep creating. Keep making things.

Whew. Okay. Glad I could get that off my chest.

There's one more monster of perfectionism I want us to outline, and this one may come as a shock to you. What does a perfectionist do when he is trying to perfect his product? He mentally, emotionally, and sometimes physically will isolate himself until his product is perfect.

There's two issues with this: first, like we've said above, perfectionism is a myth and lie, so it is never achievable. Secondly, isolation produces loneliness. And isolation and perfectionism is a horrible mix.

Let's talk about the monster of loneliness.

Creativity and loneliness seem to go hand in hand. Some even believe loneliness is essential to creativity; not only as a by-product, but also a catalyst. A study from Johns Hopkins University found that people who were socially rejected early in their life tend to be the most creative.

Basically, rejection becomes their "fuel."

This explains why creative people are usually pretty weird. They are literally "out there." On the fringe. Refusing to conform. Which can make their work meaningful, but also make their work impossible.

And this is the main reason why makers will isolate themselves. They remove themselves from society to work on their projects because only they can satisfy their hunger of perfectionism. And this can prove deadly. We need to move beyond the myth of the self-destructive genius and search for healthier approaches to sustainable creativity. To do this, we must surround ourselves with a healthy community.

Hang out with people who like to make things out of wood. Hang out with people who bake. Hang out with a guy who is really into his motorcycle. That is where real life is happening. If makers get too far removed from real life, they soon become irrelevant.

Creative people might live on the fringe, but that doesn't mean we can't find people to camp with while we're out there. It doesn't take very many, but having the right people speaking into your life and your work will make all the difference.

I recently had a conversation with my mother about the first time she saw anger and frustration out of me. I was two years old, and I would walk out of my room crying and angry. She would ask me what was wrong, and I wouldn't say anything. She said that I did this consecutively for two weeks until she figured out what was going on.

She tried to put a picture I drew on the fridge, and I told her no because it wasn't good enough. She then asked "is that the reason why you've been so angry? Because you don't like your coloring?" I was getting angry at her because I couldn't color inside the lines.

Even at the age of two, perfectionism was inside of me. And was attaching the product I could create to the value of my life.

That problem right there is the core root of perfectionism. The reason so many of us want a perfect product is because we innately want to be perfect people, and we want our product to reflect the individual value of ourselves.

That right there, is why perfectionism is flawed.

Here's the thing: we're all going to create something that is messy. We're all going to to do irrevocable things that we wish we could take back. You're going to say something that you won't agree with later. We all make decisions based on where we are in life, what we currently invest our souls into, and what drives us to stand our ground on particular subjects.

Just know that down your life path, you'll probably look back and think you screwed up. And your perfectionist spirit will hate that. *13

But here's the thing we all have to remember: we're a bunch of screw ups.

And that's cool. Because you don't have to be perfect to be who you are.

If I'm saying anything, it's this: be yourself and who you are. Don't hide your personality from other people. Stand up for what you believe in. Always do the right thing. Be passionate. Rise above the peer pressure of those around you, and live authentically. Force yourself to be who you really are.

When you look back on your life and the crazy things you said and did, you'll have a smile on your face, because even though right now you might think it was an immature act, you knew you were standing on ground on what you believed in.

In two years, I'm sure I'll look back on this book and wish I had written it differently.

That's because I'm a screw-up. And so are you.

And that's perfectly okay.

Be a screw-up.

Screw ups always win the battles against perfectionists.

Perfectionism is one of the hardest monsters you have to face as a maker. Perfectionism is the voice of oppression. Perfectionism becomes a golden trophy with you playing the part of the bloody winner.

And no one needs that.

The only person who wants you to be a perfectionist is you.

It's okay to color outside of the lines.

Your grass doesn't have to be the greenest.

I re-wrote this chapter five times, and I'm still not happy with it.

I also left seven grammar errors in it on purpose.

To hell with you, monster of perfectionism.

CHAPTER EIGHT:
Whispers and Chaos

I'll never forget the day I had my first panic attack.

I was sitting in a class in college when all of a sudden, my heart started pounding uncontrollably. I immediately clenched the sides of my desk, focusing on every beat of my heart. My eyes started watering and my face went numb. I became extremely dizzy. My hands were cold, and my face was beat red.

I got up in the middle of class. I left all my belongings at my desk and walked out as fast as I could.

"Just get to your dorm and call a doctor. Just get there fast. You're going to be okay."

I started walking as fast as I could to get out of the building. Then, out of nowhere, halfway down the hallway, my heartbeat calmed. I could see clearly. I stopped sweating. And it felt like everything was back to normal.

Two minutes ago, I thought I was dying. And here I was, standing in the middle of a vacant hallway, wondering to myself, "what just happened?"

Little did I know, this was the beginning of my relationship with panic and anxiety disorder. And this was the first panic attack of many to follow. I spent the next 2 months in and out of hospitals and emergency rooms. I was making daily doctor calls. I would start having what I thought was another heart attack, and I would end up in a doctors office only for them to tell me my heartbeat was perfectly fine and I was most likely having a panic attack.

I didn't believe them. I convinced myself something physically was wrong. I mean, why would I be having panic attacks? Why would this start, and why now?

The panic attacks were so bad that I had to leave college and move back home to Indiana. They even got to a point where I wasn't able to leave the house. I started having them more frequently. More severe. In every facet, they were controlling my every move.

I spent a total of 43 days in my house without leaving in fear that a panic attack would happen in public.

43 days.

I felt like a complete failure of a person. And that's when the depression sank in.

Here's the biggest secret that I have: I am a pastor that deals with anxiety and panic disorder.

If you're not familiar with the term, let me explain it to you: panic disorder is when you have reoccurring unexpected panic attacks. They are sudden periods of intense feelings that you simply can't control. Your body goes into full-blown overdrive, and you feel like what I would think a heart attack feels like.

I thought having panic attacks were bad: the depression that followed was an entirely different story. Depression hits humans in various ways. For some people, depression is an everyday battle. For others, it comes and goes in waves.

Here's the good news: through correct medication, proper mental awareness, honesty about my illness, and having the right support, I was able to battle anxiety and panic disorder, and ultimately take back my life from its controlling power. And ever since then, I've tried to keep this part of my life under the radar.

It was as if letting people in on this guilt-ridden topic would in some way decline my value to them as a person. I spent years feeling like there this big stain on my integrity because of my illness.

It hasn't been until recently that I realized the power of letting in other people to see your monsters.

It hasn't been until recently that I realized my monsters are the exact same monsters others fight.

In this chapter, we are going to look at one of the most hidden monsters that more than most makers face: depression and anxiety.

Some of us have finally learned to be okay with letting people into the dark corners of our lives and let them know that we deal with depression and anxiety. However, there's still a group of makers that hide their civil war with this monster.. And that group isn't small.

There are 311 million people living in America, and 253 million of those people in some way were prescribed medication for panic disorder, anxiety, or depression last year.

According to the CDC, 1 in 10 Americans has claimed to suffer from some form of depression. Every year, that equates to more than 7% of us having to suffer from agonizing loneliness, mental and emotional darkness, and numerous other symptoms of varying degrees all attributed to this singular, albeit broad by definition, disorder: depression. But for some reason, creatives are singled out more often than not when it comes to depression. [14]

Also, before we dig in, please understand that in no way am a doctor or am I prescribing you a certain medication or a scientifically proven position on this topic. I am simply giving you the answers I received, my personal history, and leadership I have had through my personal battle with depression.

Maybe you are a maker who doesn't deal with depression and anxiety. As we've learned in chapters past, being a maker means leaving a legacy of leadership. If you are the maker God intends for you to be, there is a solid chance you're going to be put in a leadership position where you're going to help someone who is battling this monster.

And for the makers that live with this monster of depression and anxiety, please understand, you are not alone in your fight.

I'll say it again, you are not alone.

Monsters like perfectionism, lack of balancing your work load, and even holding onto toxic relationships and friendships are all triggers for depression. As a matter of fact, the maker who lives with depression will probably tell you that all his other monsters came together and morphed into one big monster called Depression. The monsters we outlined in the previous chapters are triggers than can cause a maker to meet the monster of depression, anxiety, and panic disorder.

Here's the weird thing though. I feel like makers who live their lives to create from their influences are always the ones that are singled out for having depression. Somewhere between van Gogh cutting his ear off and Virginia Woolf walking into a river, we got the idea that true artists are tortured artists.

I get it. Some of the world's most brilliant minds were troubled, and because of this, some of us start thinking that mental illness must be the key ingredient to creativity.

Some of my most authentic work has come from a place when I am feel like there is nothing else to do but create.

I love old western movies. One of my favorite's is one of Clint Eastwood's move iconic westerns called *The Outlaw Josey Wales.* There's one particular scene where Josey Wales (Clint Eastwood) looks at his counter-part (Sondra Locke) and says,

"When you are backed up into a corner and got no where to go, you've only got one option Break down the damn wall."

Maker: when depression and anxiety has backed us up into a wall, what do we do?

We grab our paint brush. Our guitars. Our notebooks.

We create. We create, because there is no where else for us to go, and there is nothing else left to do.

We create.

And we break down the damn wall.

The stereotype of the tortured artist suggests we create better work while we are depressed or struggling.

Here's the hardest part for any maker who has lived a life of darkness with depression: living with anxiety and depression is one of the hardest mental and emotional illnesses that a person can feel; but some of our greatest work happens when we're in our lowest points.

This is the dichotomy of the maker riddled with depression: I call it the "Wendigo Effect."

The Curse of the Wendigo was a book written by Richard Covey, an adult horror novelist. The book takes us on a journey of a man who studies monsters for a living, called a Monstrumologist. The Monstrumologist comes across this monster that is called The Wendigo, which is a monster who craves and eats human flesh, but at the same time, as soon as he consumes human flesh, his body starts to starve itself.

The maker who creates from his darkness suffers from The Wendigo Effect. Depression can be the worst feeling we feel, yet, we always know that we will create something out of it. And while it may not happen during our spout of depression, once our mind clears up, we begin to create from our current past of our darkness.

And this is why makers can be so obsessed with the mad genius? Because at the core of every mad genius, their content is created from The Wendigo Effect.

The negativity bias is at play here. By nature, humans are more affected by negativity than positivity. It's why gossip travels fast. It's why everything in the news seems depressing. Humans crave dramatic stories.

Our obsession with negativity is programmed into us. For example: what seems to trigger more notice: a banana, or a tiger running towards you at 110mph? Of course, the tiger, because it presents a threat. And a threat is a negative situation.

However, maker, please understand that while depression can drive your creativity, it should not be in the drivers seat all the time.

Nancy Andreasen, the author of "The Creating Brain: The Neuroscience of Genius," conducted studies and interviews to understand the brains of geniuses, including the relationship between creativity and mental illness.

"Although many writers had had periods of significant depression, mania, or hypomania, they were consistently appealing, entertaining, and interesting people. They had led interesting lives, and they enjoyed telling me about them as much as I enjoyed hearing about them,"

Andreasen writes, "….They were also able to describe how abnormalities in mood state affected their creativity. Consistently, they indicated that they were unable to be creative when either depressed or manic."

As human beings, we will always experience suffering at points in our life. Reflecting on dark times may even add an edge to our art or fuel the inspiration for a project. But we should not seek struggle for the sake of creativity.

So when, what should we do? How do we find the balance between creating from the dark and the light?

I personally believe that we have that we *need* to reject the darkness. Maker: what would it look like for you to reject this stereotype and the negativity that's attached to it? Instead, find variety in your work. Push yourself out of your comfort zone, but don't push yourself over the edge.

Pursue happiness and not content creation. And I think overtime, you'll be able to find balance between creating from the darkness, and living in the light.

And while I know this isn't some 3-step plan to overcoming depression (because such a thing does not exist), I think managing and balancing the time we spend in our depression is key.

The question is not making a life out of art is stressful. It's how you're going to deal with the stress when it inevitably comes your way. Stress is a physiological survival mechanism. It's our body's way of telling us to run away from dinosaurs and hide in a cave. But it's also philosophical. Some of the most productive, well-respected makers in the world deal with stress on a daily basis. And they've learned how to put it in its place.

I feel stress a pretty good amount of the time. It comes with the territory of being a pastor. Pastoring involves so many relationships and dynamics, so it's just inevitable.

The trick is to be aware of it, and knowing how to manage it.

Building up a community around myself that allows me to not only manage my stress, but to push myself into new and dangerous creative territory has been one of the greatest assets in my pastoring. Without people to connect and collaborate with, I'd probably be dead.

Maker: your community around you, especially the people who you collaborating with on your greatest inventions will be the people that hold your hand during your stress and depression. For you to create from the dark places in your life while also living in the light, you must create that community around you that won't let you create alone.

Stress is this deep-rooted intuitive thing where we can feel it bubbling to the surface from afar, but there's a tremendous value to stress. Stress can let you know you're on the right path and that you're pushing past your comfort zone.

If If I didn't have the community that I have around me, I'm certain I'd either be living in a cabin in the woods, or I'd be a completely jaded 27-year-old musician and writer. Neither of those options sounds like fun to me.

Well, the cabin idea is intriguing. But I'd probably become that hermit-cabin guy that everyone in the village is scared of because he never bathes or shaves.

Moving on.

If you are a maker who lives with depression, then please understand, while depression may be dark, the color of depression is not black.

Because of depression, you get all of these different colors of life around you all the time, You feel more. You see more.

Also creating from your dark side can be dangerous. Don't put all of that pressure on your art form. It's important to have deep relationships with friends and family with whom you frequently connect. Without that, it's very easy to come to a breaking point in your art form.

Nobody wants to or should be alone. Just like an unborn child with an umbilical cord, we need other to ease our suffering and to survive. We crave true connection. The world is a crazy place, and it can be very dangerous for an isolated soul. There's always going to be something we can stress about.

Learning to manage stress is such an important skill in a makers life, but the management of stress is only half the battle. Maker: if you are one of the blessed who deal with depression, anxiety, and any amount of sadness, know that you can turn this monster into one of the greatest tools on your tool belt.

For many years, I would ask God, "why did you do this to me?" And when I learned to accept this monster, it turned into one of the greatest assets of a maker.

Some of the greatest artists in the world are the ones who have the most scars. Depression, panic, and anxiety, is a big scar on my life. But the life lessons, creations, and leadership I have developed because of it has catapulted me years beyond where I could be as a maker.

Embrace your depression.

Embrace your monsters.

Make things out of scars.

CHAPTER NINE:

The War is Over

I wasn't a jock or a nerd.. I wasn't part of the AV club, I didn't hang out with the emo kids, and I wasn't on the chess team. I was in this weird sub-category. I guess you can call it the "forgotten" group. I was a pretty quiet kid for the most part, outside of the handful of times I was talking back to my art teacher. I spent my days coloring outside of the lines and writing books about mice. I was a huge daydreamer. I spent a lot of time roaming around my little farm town, doing everything from riding my bike up long lost dirt roads to creating slingshots out of rubber bands and broken pieces of wood.

But as I grew up and my emotions matured, the rumination of my childhood would turn into mixed emotions that would send me a downward spiral into depression.

I had a mother who loved me unconditionally and a stepfather who took the reigns of leadership in our household. I didn't know anything about my biological father. But growing up, there was always a feeling a loneliness. This wasn't brought on by anyone else, but I always felt like something was missing.

It was a weird feeling that I can't even explain today. I was alone, and even though I felt okay with being alone, I felt this void in my life. As I walked into my early 20's, I still felt that there was a part of my past that I wasn't aware of, or a segment of my story I had never experienced.

On a hot summer day in Indiana, I received a phone call from an unknown number that would change everything in my life.

"Hi, Josh. This is your half-brother."

For a second, I thought it was a joke a friend was playing on me or just someone trying to mess with me. But after a few minutes, I realized two things: I have a brother, and I'm talking to him on the phone, right now.

I stood on the other side of the phone call completely numb. We had a 10 minute discussion, almost as if both of us were trying to cram everything from the last 20 years into one short phone call.

Not much came out of our time together, except for one piece of information: he gave me my biological fathers phone number.

I remember sitting my car, looking at this piece of paper with a phone number on it - a phone number that could answer so many questions. A phone number that could help me fill this gap I had felt for years. A phone number that could change everything.

It took me 13 days to finally call the number.

The first time I called, it rang a number times until finally going to voicemail.

It was during that voicemail that I heard my biological fathers voice for the first time.

It had this deep "working mans" tone. It sounded rugged, like someone who was tired but also had a bit of an edge to it.

I left him a voicemail and moved on with my day.

Two weeks went by, and I had heard nothing. And to be honest, I completely forgot about the situation. I went on with my life as usual.

Until one day, I received a voicemail back.

It was my father's voice. I'll never forget what the voicemail said:

"Hi, Josh. This is your dad. I'm sure you'd like to meet, I sure would like that too. Call me back, son."

"Son."

For some reason, him calling me "son" made the entire situation monstrous to my heart.

I called him back, and we made plans to meet that night at his house. I spent the entire day preparing for what I would talk about. I had so many questions, and I knew he could answer them.

And if anything, I just wanted that void in my heart to be mended. I just wanted to feel closure to my past that was unknown to me.

It was about a 15 minute drive to his house. It was pitch black outside as I walked up to his door and rang the doorbell.

No answer.

I ran the doorbell three more times, with no answer.

"He ditched me. I can't believe it. He totally ditched me."

Almost immediately, anger started pouring into my heart.

I decided to do some research on my own about him. I found out that he owned a construction company and lived on a farm that sold wheat and corn. I also found out that the address he gave me wasn't his house. As a matter of fact, his real house was less than a five minute drive from where I grew up. It took me a while to comprehend that my biological father had lived less than five minutes from me for over two decades and he never reached out to me.

So many emotions at this point were hitting me. And then one day, they boiled over to where I couldn't stand it anymore.

I drove to his house…his real house, knocked on his door and waited. There were four different cars parked in the driveway, so I knew someone had to be there.

I waited over 15 minutes and heard nothing.

I walked out to his barn behind the house to see if anyone was there. I saw no one.

It wasn't until I was walking back to my car that I heard the door to a small shed across the yard open.

And there stood my biological father.

It took me a second to comprehend that this was finally happening.

We shook hands. He had a strong handshake. He was tall and had broad shoulders. His face was worn.

"Joshua, I assume."

"Yes."

"Come into my office and we'll chat for a bit."

I walked into a shed that was converted into a makeshift office for his construction company. It reeked of alcohol and cigarette smoke. The lights were off, outside of a small desk lamp and natural light spilling in from a window.

He spoke first.

"Well…what do you want to know?"

I had so many questions, and now that the time was here, I wasn't sure where to even begin.

We talked about jobs. Upbringings. Small talk.

Finally, he just looked at me and said, "well, why are you really here? Do you need money? Or what?"

It was then that I flat out asked him the biggest question I had been wondering for years.

"Honestly, I just want to know one thing: why didn't you want me?"

I'll never forget his response.

He chuckled.

He actually chuckled.

"Well, that's a loaded question. There were a lot of things that happened that you don't know about. But if you want the truth, I'll tell you: you were too big of a burden to bear."

That was pretty much the end of the conversation. As I walked out, I turned around and said, "I have questions, and I need answers. You may not want a relationship with me, but what I need right now is answers."

I think he found my persistence admirable.

A jaded smirk came across his face.

"Let's do this again. I sure would like that."

We decided two weeks from that day to meet again.

I left that day feeling one feeling I wasn't expecting: hope.

However, six days later, I got news that completely turned my world upside down. I received a phone call from someone whom I'll leave anonymous.

"Hi Josh. Are you sitting down? I need to tell you something."

I immediately knew something was wrong.

"Your dad killed himself last night."

Six days after I met my father, he committed suicide.

Anger and depression immediately flooded my soul. I was overwhelmed with so many emotions. I didn't even know what my next step in life would now be. This man was supposed to answer all the questions that were inside of me for years. And now, I would never know the answers to those questions.

I was scared.

I was mad.

I was lost.

What I didn't realize was that Jesus had just catapulted me into the biggest experience I would ever have as a maker.

What does total dependence really mean? I had been in the church world for so long that this phrase was just numb to me. What I learned through this situation was this: I was relying on an outside source to fill who I was. An outside source to answer all of my questions. An outside source to tell me who I was.

When my biological father died, I became a producing machine. I would work out twice a day. Spend hours writing. Making phone calls to clients. Working endlessly from sun up to sun down.

I would be a liar if I said I hated it. As a matter of fact, I loved every minute of it. Because it made me forget that I ever had any encounter with my biological father. Every ounce of my life consisted of me producing something…something that would make me feel validated and wanted by others.

About a month into this new cycle of work, I woke up one day with the flu. And it scared me, because I knew I wouldn't be able to work at the level I had been working.

Drowning myself in my work was the only I knew to remove the pain of my fathers passing. And while laying in bed, riddled with a fever, Jesus finally brought my selfishness to my attention.

This was the first time in my life that I realized that I was relying on my experiences, situations, and dreams to create.

And what I had left out was The Original Maker.

And that I was my worst enemy.

Friends: if we leave The Original Maker out of our creations, our creations will have no lasting legacy, because they are created on sinking sand. And this is exactly what I was doing. I was literally hiding from Jesus behind my work. I wanted the control. I didn't want to believe that Jesus could fulfill me. I wanted my earthly father to do that. I wanted my products to do that.

But I quickly learned that I would fall short every time I tried to take the reigns over my own life.

Monsters fascinate me. There's something in the shadows that you don't understand. You can't quite make out the shape of it. It's something that can eat you. Something that can steal your children, spoil your crops, or worst of all turn you into a monster yourself, so that you'll no longer be welcome in the warm places where we tell stories about monsters.

Throughout this book, we've talked about finding your inner artist as a maker and fighting your inner critic which are your monsters.

But there is one monster we haven't discussed yet. And it's the biggest monster of them all.

You.

You are the biggest monster of them all.

While we've discussed several different monsters in this book, they all come back full circle: they are created by your individuality. They are monsters that the makers create.

But here's the beautiful thing about the damage we create through our monsters: **Jesus is the greatest Maker of them all,** and He has already conquered our monsters for us.

Friends: listen to me. You and I both know that you have had trouble in your life. And that trouble intensifies from season to season. Difficulty is an inescapable aspect of living in a cursed world. And whether your are a CEO of a thriving business, a starving artist in San Francisco, or a stay-at-home mother with 4 screaming children, we all feel like we fall short in some capacity.

But there are glimpses of goodness to be seen and joyful experiences to be had.

God's common grace ensures that life is not a long sequence of monstrous events. Maker: the love of Jesus feels the pains of our monsters the most. The Holy Spirit has introduced to our souls to a foretaste of the perfect, heavenly world that has been created in the image of our Creator.

As we experience in small measure the creativity of Jesus in our human design, we groan with eager longing for the day when Jesus breaks through the clouds and spills his curse-destroying, trouble-expelling glory over all the earth. But until then, our monsters will grow and become even more powerful.

And if our monsters grow ever more powerful? What does the maker do in response?

We fight. We endure the trouble. We entrust ourselves to The Maker, knowing that his grace is sufficient to sustain us and that our hearts will find His comfort and love to be enough. Those battles turn into refinement for the maker, and gives us the authority and authenticity to create our masterpieces.

Friends, I understand this is easier said than done.

To be honest, there are times I don't feel secure enough to say those things with confidence. Trying to find rest in my biological father was a time when I completely ignored the saving power of Jesus and only focused on the monster in front of me. We all have times where we worry that Jesus won't sustain us or when our hearts fail to find comfort in all that He is. That's when we ask ourselves "Will he really sustain me? Will he really be enough for me?"

Maker: He will absolutely sustain you. John 10:29 explains to us that nothing can snatch us out of the Father's hand:

Jesus answered, "I told you, but you don't believe. Everything I have done has been authorized by my Father, actions that speak louder than words. You don't believe because you're not my sheep. My sheep recognize my voice. I know them, and they follow me. I give them real and eternal life. They are protected from the Destroyer for good. No one can steal them from out of my hand. The Father who put them under my care is so much greater than the Destroyer and Thief. No one could ever get them away from him. I and the Father are one heart and mind."

And He even goes on to tell us how much He loves us, even when we don't believe Him in Romans 8:38-39:

So, what do you think? With God on our side like this, how can we lose? If God didn't hesitate to put everything on the line for us, embracing our condition and exposing himself to the worst by sending his own Son, is there anything else he wouldn't gladly and freely do for us? And who would dare tangle with God by messing with one of God's chosen? Who would dare even to point a finger? The One who died for us—who was raised to life for us!—is in the presence of God at this very moment sticking up for us. Do you think anyone is going to be able to drive a wedge between us and Christ's love for us? There is no way! Not trouble, not hard times, not hatred, not hunger, not homelessness, not bullying threats, not backstabbing, not even the worst sins listed in Scripture:

Friends, with God on our side like this, there's no chance that we can lose.

God never hesitated to put everything on the line for His children. Therefore, God created the most miraculous piece of artwork that man has ever seen: His Son, Jesus. And God exposed Jesus to the worst by sending Him to earth.

Romans 8:38-39 says,

If God didn't hesitate to put everything on the line for us, embracing our condition and exposing himself to the worst by sending his own Son, is there anything else he wouldn't gladly and freely do for us?

And who would dare tangle with God by messing with one of God's chosen? Who would dare even to point a finger?

The One who died for us—who was raised to life for us, is in the presence of God at this very moment is sticking up for us. Do you think any monster will ever be able to drive a wedge between us and Christ's love for us?

Not a chance, maker. Not a chance.

Nothing can. Nothing living, nothing dead. No monster. No depression. No hardship. Nothing thinkable or unthinkable can ever come between us and God's love.

He will throw us into the hardest fights with our monsters. And sometimes, we will lose. But friend, while we may fight these battles with ourselves each and every day, we can live with the confidence that Jesus has always won the war.

Jesus sustains us through hard times, and because of this, we can find ultimate rest and assurance in Him.

"In your presence, there is fullness of joy, at your right hand are pleasures forever more!"- Psalm 16:11.

In the presence of God, we find our ultimate strength; strength not find in what we can do, what we can produce, but solely in Him.

He gives us a strength to create. To endure pain. To manage conflict. To love more.

And all of this love finds a home in God.

"My flesh and my heart may fail, but God is the strength of my heart and my portion forever." – Psalm 73:26.

My friends: Jesus is enough.

Jesus is *more* than enough.

And this means we don't have to be good enough.

Our monsters will continue to bring times of trial and trouble, but our hearts can live in a place where we can be strong enough to defeat any enemy that comes into our lives.

And in those moments, we remember just how loved we really are.

And this is where I was when my father killed himself. And through this monster of a situation, The Maker reminded me how precious I am to Him.

Trouble hurts. Trials are unpleasant. But these monsters aren't able to lay a finger on the God-centered joy and peace that have been infused into my heart by means of my relationship with Him.

In John chapters 14-17 Jesus promises that:

His joy would be in us.

He would manifest himself to us.

He and the Father would make their home with us.

To give us His peace so that the trouble we experience in this world wouldn't trouble our hearts.

This peace is what fights our inner critic the most.

But what about our inner artist?

Our artwork can be perfectly executed and beautiful, but it can still be wasteful if we don't first begin with listening to Jesus for what we create. If our artistry isn't founded in the original Maker, it's already flawed.

So what happens when we create from the voice of Jesus and not ourselves? We end up creating beautiful pieces of artwork that we could never create ourselves.

The anointing over our creations is the x-factor behind the creator. The anointing of Jesus is fascinating. It can't be understood. He creates something that humanity is attracted to, and He uses makers as the funnel for his anointing.

Friend; humble yourself enough to understand that what you can selfishly create can never reach the level of Jesus' anointing.

As makers, our interests eventually manifests themselves into art. The first step to making anointed work is to follow the Maker. If we do this, our artwork will never be in void.

Art founded in a truthful message gets stuck in people's heads. On some level, it just clicks. Not only will our art stick with people, but the message to the masses will be more clear than ever.

So what about you, maker? Is it time for you to break your pattern of relying on yourself?

Trust me when I say, when we put our reliance in The Maker, He can quickly surprise us with just how anointed our creations can be.

Surprise is at the heart of all great creations, as long as the Maker is the heart itself. Non-impactful art can prove itself useless if we only focus on creating by ourselves. Simply put, if we create *by* ourselves, we're simply creating *for* ourselves.

And honestly guys, I'm still figuring this out. So why we don't we figure this out together? Let's throw ourselves at projects, and lean on Him as we go. There's always a high chance of failure in societies eyes when we work that way, but the greatest truth in this is this: it's already a masterpiece in the eyes of our Savior.

Maker, as we focus on who Jesus is to us as the Original Artist, we must always remember to listen to His voice, and not the voice of our monsters.

As artists who deal with inner conflicts on a daily basis, I'll be the first to admit that the "you're not good enough" monster has crept in more often than nought.

Friends, as we end this journey of finding our inner artist and fighting our inner critics, I want to leave you with words that you may not hear often. The beautiful thing is, these are words that Jesus has already told us about ourselves.

Friends, please listen to me closely.

You are not that voice that tells you "you are not worth it."

You are not that emotional pit in your stomach.

You are not your bank account.

You are not your things.

You are not that man about give up because he has lost everything.

You are not those people wanting you to give more, do more, serve more.

You are not your failures.

You are not your reached goals.

You are not the song you lead, the sermon you preach, or the person you disciple.

You are not your Facebook, Instagram, or Twitter account.

You are not that self-help book.

You are not who you see in the mirror.

You are not the person you are trying to become.

You are not the sellout.

You are not a lost wandering human.

You need to know is that you are who Jesus says you are.

You are loved.

You are His child. And He also guarantees us that He will be here for the long haul.

The thoughts in your head are not your own.

Take a ten-minute breather, come back and take care of your situation.

Today is your day to start your reboot. Get off your couch, and start living your life.

Live life to it's fullest. And sometimes, that means slowing down.

Cherish what you have.

You don't have to be the best. Just be you.

Insecurity is a lie. Your security relies in Jesus, and Jesus alone.

No, you're not a deadbeat pastor. Your flock doesn't hate you. Be shepherded by Jesus, and He will let you shepherd your people.

You don't have to do it all. Pick two things; and become a master at that.

Work hard. Work smart. But don't find your validity in how hard you work, or how smart you are. Find it in who you are, and not what you can create.

I don't care what they did; just love them back.

Stop expecting your team, family and friends to be a clone of you.

Just love.

Nothing else matters right now.

Just love.

If any of these hit home, then know you're not alone. Jesus has you. And the great thing is, He never lets us go.

You will never have all the answers to defeat your monsters.

But as a maker, you don't have to have all the answers.

You will always be a maker.

You will always be a monster.

You will never be good enough.

Because Jesus will always be more than enough.

Benediction

May you, a maker who is striving to change the world, have blessings of forward movement and gospel-driven authority in the lifeblood of your artistry. I pray that the art in you would come from the very brush of the Spirit who dwells inside of you; that everything you may touch, create, or lead would have the breath of Christ breathed upon it. May your soul, mind and heart be open to a legacy that leads those around you to create in the image of their Creator. Lead well, and I pray that your leadership would be a direct reflection of our Leader.

May you pour out everything you are into every pen stroke, typed letter, word, and song. Quietly listen for Him to breath His passion into you. Maintain a lifestyle where you are always bending, and our Creator is lifted High. I pray that your legacy would make a impact on this world.

I pray a blessing over those of you who are trying to get out of the way of yourself, and let God do a work in you. I pray blessings over your craft, that you can continue to stretch your limits in a way that can continue to pursue the high calling that is the call of Jesus Christ our Lord.

May you, maker created from the Maker, create the image that reflects grace, love, and peace to all those who will see, hear, and experience your message. May your brush be filled with creativity and flourish with devotion to your craft. May your monsters be known, fought, and recognized, as you strive to be the greatest Maker you can be.

May you, child of the one true King, continue to be a child - learning with open hearts and open eyes. I pray that you remove perfectionism from your vocabulary. Continue to celebrate your craziness. Answer the call to war towards your artistry, and also realize you have what it takes to conquer the battles. Ground yourself in those things that you know, and let go of the things you need to release in order to create in full transparency. I pray blessings over the authenticity of your creations. Create the image that dictates your personality and character.

Give away your art. Give away your platform. Invest your leadership into others who will be better Makers than you can ever be.

Maker: may you, a Child of the Maker, make much of Jesus.

Notes

1. Travis is a close friend. A brother. My pastor. But more than that, he understands *me,* and he understands *my voice.* And I couldn't have thought of a better person to write my forward. Except for Tupac. But he's dead.

2. Not really the trash, per se…but I definitely stuck that sucker in the darkest part of Dropbox that I know about. Maybe that'll be the next book?

3. Honestly ya'll, she hated me, I'm sure of it, because that snowman project was the DUMBEST thing ever. But still I'm sure like 98% of the problem was me.

4. Thanks, P! You da real MVP. Here's your cited footnote. Don't sue me.

5. If any of you have history being part with the Independent Fundamental Baptist movement, please feel free to contact me. I have come across several women and men who have been emotionally, sexually, and spiritually abused by "men of god" who feel that they are above God. I am here for you, and I hope you understand that what you saw was not Jesus.

6. Kenny Kim and his work has been showcased on MusicBed.com, which is where many of these ideas from his discussion came from.

7. Shannon Adler is a author and poet. You can find more about her at www.deseretbook.com.

8. Liz Sandal is a great friend of mine, a life coach, and a true champion of living with authenticity. Thanks for sharing these thoughts, Liz!

9. Donald, you are SO the man. Thanks for sharing, my man!

10. Okay guys....I know, I know...it's another story about my awful art teacher. Like I said before, 98% of the problem was ME. NOT HER. ME. IT WAS JOSH'S PROBLEMS BECAUSE I HAD AN AUTHORITY ISSUE WHEN I WAS LITTLE. Also, it's not my fault she was full of great artistic values that made her look bad. Hmm...maybe that was her plot the entire time. Touché art teacher, touché....

11. Andy Raskin wrote a blog on Medium about Max and his awesome theories of the Stinky Cow. These thoughts come from Max and Andy's blog posts.

12. Tobias Van Schneider is like, the raddest guy I know. These thoughts are my own, but were inspired by his amazing posts on his blog, vanschneider.com.

13. Please understand, in no way am I saying you should do this.

14. Please seek medical help from certified doctors before you choose how to embrace battling anxiety and depression.

15. Segmeister & Walsh is a NYC based design firm that has some amazing work. Many of these thoughts came from Sagmester and their company blog.

16. Mary Karr is a tremendous author, and I hope you all will read "The Art of Memoir."

About the Author

Josh White was born and raised in Noblesville, Indiana, a small farming town in the rural midwest. Even though the silent fields of Indiana hold a special place in his heart, he knew that there was more that he needed to explore. When he was 18, Josh packed up his things and moved to Northern California.

What has happened in the years since is something he'll never get over. Josh has seen truth to the verse "God is able to do immeasurably more than we can ask or imagine." He's learned that firsthand.

Josh and his wife Rachel reside in San Francisco, CA where he serves as the Worship Pastor at Canvas SF, as well as the Creative Director for The Church Collective.

More than anything, he longs for people to know, love and create in the image of The Creator.

Use Spotify?

Listen to the Makers & Monsters Playlist on Spotify. Josh wrote the words to this book while listening to the songs on this playlist.

sola fusti et nimimum diu,

et vos in me, et parietes per cicuitum

et cambered ea illuminas par esse

manifesto lampados, et ferream lusibus.

CPSIA information can be obtained
at www.ICGtesting.com
Printed in the USA
FSOW03n0735310817
38218FS